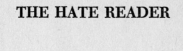

THE HATE READER

the
HATE
reader

A collection of materials on the impact of hate movements in American society, including excerpts and commentary of eminent political and social scientists.

Selected and Edited by
EDWIN S. NEWMAN
Member, New York Bar

OCEANA PUBLICATIONS, INC.
Dobbs Ferry, New York
1964

CREDITS AND ACKNOWLEDGMENTS

The editor is deeply indebted to the following authors, publishers and periodicals for permission to reprint the items herein excerpted.

The American Jewish Committee and Harper & Brothers for excerpts from the "Studies in Prejudice" Series, specifically, *Dynamics of Prejudice* by Bruno Bettelheim and Morris Janowitz; *Anti-Semitism and Emotional Disorder* by Nathan W. Ackerman and Marie Jahoda; *Prophets of Deceit* by Leo Lowenthal and Norbert Guterman. Copyright, 1950, by the American Jewish Committee.

S. Andhil Fineberg and Doubleday and Company for excerpt from *Punishment without Crime*. Copyright, 1949 by S. Andhil Fineberg.

Dr. Muzafer Sherif and Scientific American for excerpted article, "Experiments in Group Conflict," November, 1956.

The American Jewish Committee for the excerpted pamphlet "Why the Swastika?" by staff member, Ann G. Wolfe, January, 1962.

The Anti-Defamation League of B'nai B'rith for the excerpts from pamphlet, "Swastika 1960" by David Coplovitz and Candace Rogers, Copyright, 1961 by the Anti-Defamation League of B'nai B'rith.

The Anti-Defamation League of B'nai B'rith for its excerpted issue of its monthly publication, "Facts," October, 1963.

The American Jewish Committee for the excerpted fact sheet For Your Information, "Report on the Black Muslims," July, 1963.

The National Association of Intergroup Relations Officials and its Journal of Intergroup Relations for the excerpted article, "Deflating the Professional Bigot," by S. Andhil Fineberg, January, 1960.

The New York Times Magazine for the excerpted articles, "The Negro Child Asks: Why?" by Margaret Anderson, December 1, 1963; and "What Kind of Nation Are We?" by Andrew Hacker, December 8, 1963.

231433

Beacon Press and Kenneth B. Clark for the excerpt from his interview with Rev. Martin Luther King from *The Negro Protest*. Copyright, 1963, by Kenneth B. Clark.

James Baldwin for selected excerpts from *The Fire Next Time*. Copyright, 1963 by James Baldwin.

Daniel Bell and Doubleday and Company for the several articles excerpted from *The Radical Right*, specifically: "The Pseudo-Conservative Revolt" by Richard Hofstadter; "The Sources of the Radical Right" by Seymour Martin Lipsett; "The Dispossessed—1962" by Daniel Bell; "The Revolt against the Elite" by Peter Viereck. Copyright, 1963, by Daniel Bell.

Commentary Magazine and Alan F. Westin for the excerpted article, "The John Birch Society, Fundamentalism on the Right." August, 1961.

The editor wishes to acknowledge specially the cooperation of the American Jewish Committee and the Anti-Defamation League, both of which represent perhaps the most extensive source of materials and analyses on hate literature and hate movements in American life. Ralph Bass of the staff of the American Jewish Committee was particularly helpful to the editor in selecting many of the items herein incorporated.

The editor wishes also to pay tribute to editor Daniel Bell and Doubleday and Company for the deeply significant volume, *The Radical Right* which, in the editor's view, is an outstanding contribution to contemporary American social psychology and political science.

The editor is also pleased to acknowledge the contribution of his son, Scott Newman, whose concept of the role of psychology in altering human relations, is indicative of the fact that the research of a decade and a half ago is beginning now to shape the thinking of tomorrow's opinion moulders.

TABLE OF CONTENTS

Section III

THE POLITICS OF HATE

INTRODUCTION

We are living in an era of social revolution in American life, and there is no doubt that its mercurial character has a shock-impact on all of us. Suddenly plunged into the space age—one aspect of which has been the development of weapons that can, in minutes, wipe out our civilization—the world seems to crowd in upon us. Abroad, we are engaged in a titanic struggle—sometimes hot, sometimes cold—against an enemy system and philosophy that is the very opposite of our own democratic traditions. Set in the context of rising nationalism among the newly free and largely colored peoples of the world, we find that the traditional weapons of big-power politics are as outmoded as would be a dinosaur in the streets.

It is not an easy concept to grasp, nor a pleasant fact to live with. But America can no longer (nor can the Soviet Union, for that matter) brandish a "big stick" and thereby maintain world-wide loyalty and discipline. As we grope through trial and error toward a realistic way of asserting ourselves, and more particularly, our ideals, in the *weltpolitik*, not all of us are able to make the adjustments. It is too, too easy to cast the mind back to a less troubled, more leisurely day—although God only knows when that was—and to seek answers to today's needs in terms of formulas and dogmas that may have had meaning for their day, but have present value only to the extent that they can be flexibly adapted to current problems. There are those of us who are unable to make the adjustments, and as a result, become part of a new "lost generation,"—rootless, insecure, unable to cope with the demands of today's living on our shrunken planet—and as a result, too ready to blame and accuse others for ills that are a product of the times.

Nor are the metes and bounds of the social revolution drawn only abroad. We are involved in an inner circle social revolution within our own borders, and again it is bound up with factors and events that are in a perpetual state of flux. The social mobility of American society, one of our prized assets, contributes to rootlessness. In a society that has fundamentally rejected class and caste, each of us looks elsewhere for identifications. The result has been a tendency toward introversion and "in-group" association, the manifestations of which are too often bigotry, prejudice and discrimination against those thought to constitute the "out-group." Tacitly accepted for so long as simply a fact of American life, discrimination has now emerged as probably the most significant domestic social issue of our times, and already quite the most violent.

One is reminded, as the struggle against Negro segregation and inequality unfolds, of a generation ago, when another revolution preoccupied the American domestic scene—the attempt of organized labor to assert its rights and position in American society. Certainly, the legal and social action pattern was similar —restrictive laws on the books that needed to be voided; new laws to protect rather than inhibit rights; court decisions in aid of the assertion of constitutional rights; and massive social action (non-violent in concept, but quite violent in its impact on the country's nervous system). In those days, it was the rights of labor; today it is the right of minority groups, and particularly, the Negro to first class citizenship as an American, with all that implies for equality of opportunity in our society.

As the revolution has asserted itself, it has been bitterly opposed by those who sense that a way of living is being destroyed. These are the same type of people who long for "the good old days," people who resist the inevitable by clinging to what they personally require in order to make some adjustment to life. Almost necessarily, they are people who must resort to hate and violence as weapons.

But they are not the only ones. There is a vast middle grouping of people—quick to mouth the shibboleths of democratic equality, but deadly afraid to see it realized. These are the subtle victims and perpetrators of prejudice, the people who are quick to criticize bigotry in the South, but who will find ample rationalization for not wanting their children to sit in classrooms with Negro youngsters in the North. They, too, are part of the hate pattern, perhaps more insidiously so than those whose commitment leaves no question where they stand.

Because the combination of an uncertain outside world and a seething domestic society leaves all but a few of us as potential prey to hate, prejudice and scapegoating as seeming solutions to our problems, this Hate Reader has been conceived. It is an attempt to detail the psychological processes by which prejudiced reactions are formed and projected, how they are utilized by clever manipulators of human feelings to create a "hate" atmosphere, and how, with refinements, these processes become the basis of a political movement.

In the choice of materials, two major sources have been utilized. Because anti-Semitism is perhaps the oldest and best documented example of prejudice, much useful material has emerged from the experience of American Jewish organizations in dealing with the phenomenon. This material and experience, which has come to be part of university scholarship in the last fifteen years, stands now applicable and available to all problems of intergroup relationships. The second major source includes the commentaries and observations of several of the country's leading political scientists, men who are keen and frank analysts of contemporary America and who demonstrate an understanding of the psychological currents in American life as well as the socio-economic currents.

It has been the editor's purpose in analyzing the role played by hate and prejudice in American life—perhaps, even dramatizing it—to contribute to knowledge of an enemy as strong and inexorable as any antagonistic system or society.

PROLOGUE

There have always been two traditions in American society. The first—and the one of which we tend collectively to be proud —is that of a nation dedicated to the goals of freedom and individual dignity. It was this tradition which I sought to define in the context of current problems and the contemporary scene in THE FREEDOM READER (1st ed., 1955; 2nd ed., 1962). And a very real and meaningful tradition it is! American democratic ideals are by no means frozen into platitudes that are part of documents of another day. With each passing day, our society as a whole honestly tries to forge a more perfect union, a more perfect democracy, on the anvil of challenges that do not seem to yield to good intentions. And like the history of mankind itself, we seem to make progress slowly—perhaps too slowly.

One reason may be that there is in American life a second tradition—equally as deeply ingrained as our quest for a practicing freedom. This tradition is not so easily defined. It is not precisely a matter of good against evil, of right against wrong. Were it that simple, we might have less difficulty in steering a straight course. It is a tradition which breeds evil—but the evil is more a symptom or a symbol. For want of a better catchword, I call it "rootlessness." It is for the weak in mind or heart or spirit the opposite side of the coin from the equalitarian aspects of America, with its emphasis on social mobility, its rejection of predetermined class or caste, its free market place of ideas, and its *laissez faire* approach to matters of religion and culture.

I use the word "rootless" in its psychological sense. The person who is or feels himself outside the mainstream of American life will seek security—an anchor—in association or identification with extremism. By definition, extremism does not seek answers to problems within the framework of democratic methods. Indeed, by definition it does not seek answers to problems at all. Rather, it seeks to articulate the problems, and to attract a following not by reason of proffered solutions, but rather by finding some one or some thing to blame. The ideology, therefore, emerges as *hate* —a weapon with which the rootless can translate their insecurities into action,—hatred of people, of groups, of institutions, of leaders —often camouflaged in the shibboleths and lexicon of democratic ideals.

It may seem rather singular that *hate* is set up as the antonym of *freedom*. The more usual connotation would invoke concepts like *slavery, repression, totalitarianism*. Yet, as we analyze American history, it becomes readily apparent that the tradition of freedom in its ever-contending battle for supremacy has faced as its major antagonist the tradition of hate—from the Know-Nothings of a hundred years ago to the American Protective Association of the eighties to the Ku Klux Klan of the twenties and the native fascist movements of the thirties; to McCarthyism and the so-called "Radical Right" among current phenomena. These are all movements whose dominant credo has not been that they are "for" something, but rather that they are "against."

It would be easy to say that these forces have been in contention since time immemorial, and that it is at best a posture to claim that the American experience is more unique in this regard than, perhaps, the European experience. Indeed, it will readily be pointed out that America was founded and built by those who rebelled against the triumph of hate in European society and sought and found the atmosphere of freedom on these shores. True, but it is this very American process which has helped to sharpen the conflict.

European society, by the very nature of its restrictions, by its clearcut distinctions of class and caste, gave people an identification. Even as political democracy came to the fore in Europe, the very politics reflected the lines of class and caste—Labor parties, Peasant parties, Catholic Worker parties, etc. Groups could and did vie for political power, without feeling the need to alter the social structure. (Actually, even in Europe today, social mobility is increasing—but it is occurring in violation of tradition, not as a part of it.) In America, from the beginnings, social mobility has been at the core of our democracy. And while it represents an advanced social process, it is not without its problems—in the same way, for example, as race relations in the Deep South were less of a problem when white supremacy was the accepted norm than today, when the Negroes no longer accept it.

Social mobility has brought with it eternal contention and conflict between the *deja arrivés* and the *arrivistes*. The descendants of the landed gentry of an earlier day resent the fact that their lineage and background do not assure their power or status. Thus, Anglo-Saxon Protestants resented the coming of Irish Catholics and, together, they resented the coming of Jews and Italians and Eastern Europeans, and all, in turn, as "white Americans" resent the strivings of the Negroes and so-called "non-whites." And for those who strive and succeed, they reject the backgrounds that spawned them in their personal search for "Americanism,"—a sort of Holy Grail that people would like to reach out and touch. It is these strivings and the inter- and intra-group conflicts that emerge from them that create the rootlessness in American society. Unlike the European who tends to accept and even feel secure in his group identification, the American aspires constantly for mobility upwards.

Political and social scientists have recently devoted much thought to this aspect of the *American way*. They point out that one need not be born an American to become one, and that this creates in many a reservoir of self-doubt. Even while tolerance is advertised as a virtue of American life, conformity and intolerance of variations from it is, in effect, the standard. Thus, we have the phenomenon that only in America, do we have concepts such as "Americanism," or "un-American activities." How often has one heard of actions in a European country described as "un-French," or "un-British" or "un-Greek." The point seems to be that the very mobility of our society creates gnawing doubts as to our national identification and loyalty, with the result that the very insecurities about our being that are thus bred become the basis for super-patriotism, ultra-conformity and fear, distrust and hatred of anything that does not fit in with a predetermined and unchanging definition of "Americanism."

These insecurities and self-doubts, this deliberate isolation from roots, this tendency to reject everything in our "non-American" culture or background contribute toward the perpetuation of this other tradition in American life—the tradition of isolationism, of provincialism, of psychological snobbery, of bigotry and prejudice —of hate!

It is this other tradition that the pages which follow will seek to explore. In putting these materials together, I have deliberately avoided yielding to the temptation to put on these pages the purple prose of professional hatemongers. Rather, the intent has been to analyze the individual and group social and psychological processes that give being to hate as a political philosophy. The work moves from a study of the dynamics of prejudice, to the methods utilized by agitators and rabblerousers to popularize hate movements to an examination of the politics of hate—as typified in contemporary America by the Radical Right. Little attempt has been made to suggest corrective or remedial action, although the social science of community relations has evolved in the last twenty years to the status of a highly disciplined profession. But the answers, if indeed, there are answers, are best reserved for another volume.

SECTION I

THE DYNAMICS OF PREJUDICE

"*If the Tiber overflows into the city,*
if the Nile does not flow into the countryside,
if the heavens remain unmoved,
if the earth quakes,
if there is famine or pestilence,
at once, the cry goes up:

To the Lions with the Christians!"

Tertullian

THE DYNAMICS OF PREJUDICE

Scapegoating is a technique literally as old as recorded history. Indeed, it derives its very name from the ancient practice of countering evils and ill-fortunes by sacrificing a goat in appeasement of wrathful gods. As society became increasingly mature— "civilized," if you will—the concept of scapegoating became more sophisticated. Human beings who, either from choice, conviction or pure happenstance of birth, found themselves as part of unpopular groups, replaced the goats, and the practice emerged of attributing to these "humans-in-lieu-of-goats" all of the misfortunes of society. America itself has been in many ways the product of scapegoating as the persecuted of the old world fled to these shores in search of freedom. But then America gradually developed its own scapegoats—Irish, Italians, foreign born, Jews, Negroes,—to such an extent that it can truly be said that the American heritage of freedom and individual dignity has always had to contend with a less savory tradition—of provincialism, prejudice, discrimination and hate.

Soberly, but dramatically, the tragic death of President Kennedy caught Americans up in the horrific realization that hate is all too rampant in this great and good land. Indeed, many prominent American leaders articulated the equation of the crazed act of a sick and frustrated individual with the underlying mood of hatred that had insinuated itself into the very roots of American human relations.

Said Chief Justice of the Supreme Court, Earl Warren, "What a price we pay for this fanaticism! . . . If we really love this country, if we truly love justice and mercy, if we fervently want to make this nation better for those who are to follow us, we can at least abjure the hatred that consumes people, the false accusations that divide us and the bitterness that begets violence."

And from Richard M. Nixon, the former vice president, "The greatest tribute we can pay to his memory is in our everyday lives to do everything we can to reduce the forces of hatred which drive men to such terrible deeds."

· Dean Francis Sayre of the Washington Cathedral, "By our readiness to allow evil to be called good and good evil; by our continued toleration of ancient injustices . . . we have all had a part in the assassination."

Walter Lippman, prominent columnist and student of the foreign scene wrote, "We must remember that democracy consists not only of liberty and equality, but of fraternity as well."

The mood of the nation was perhaps best captured in the remarks of President Lyndon B. Johnson in his 1963 Thanksgiving Day message, ". . . And how much better it would be, how much more sane it would be, how much more decent an America it would be if all Americans could spend their fortunes and give their time and spend their energies helping our system and its servants to solve your problems instead of pouring out the venom and the hate that stalemate us in progress? . . . Let us today renew our dedication to the ideals that are American. Let us pray for His divine wisdom in banishing from our land any injustice or intolerance or oppression to any of our fellow Americans whatever their opinion, whatever the color of their skins—for God made all of us, not some of us, in his image. All of us, not just some of us, are his children. . . ."

It will readily be perceived that any postitive effort to counter and conquer the hatred that can poison and destroy our society must begin in an understanding of why people hate, how their anxieties, frustrations and insecurities are exploited by hate-mongers, and how the forces of good in our society can be mobilized to isolate and eliminate the disease of hate.

THE PATTERNS OF PREJUDICE

A major contribution to the scientific approach to the problem has been a series of works published in the late forties under the title, "Studies in Prejudice." Sponsored by the American Jewish Committee, which for nearly sixty years has been dedicated to the continuing fight against prejudice and discrimination, these studies, by isolating the psychological factors in prejudiced behavior have helped point the way toward understanding and amelioration.

The several excerpts which follow attempt to define prejudice in the context of group hostility. The first is from *Dynamics of Prejudice* by Bruno Bettelheim and Morris Janowitz; the second *Anti-Semitism and Emotional Disorder* by Nathan W. Ackerman and Marie Jahoda. Both volumes are part of the "Studies in Prejudice" Series.

Group Hostility

Hostilities among groups—nations, classes, ethnic groups, or families—are alike in being directed by members of one group against those of another group in the name of certain collective symbols of identification. Such group hostility can thrive very well alongside of friendly, even intimate, relations between individuals of the two hostile groups, the accepted individual being considered an exception to his group. It is true that in many important respects the kinds of hostility among social groups differ widely. The particular goals that groups strive for, the particular social contexts in which they interact, all affect the forms of hostility. But if human behavior is to be understood and explained, the principles of group hostility in general must be determined. In other words, it is necessary to formulate and establish propositions which will cover the whole range of intergroup hostility and which will have a generalized explanatory value, even though they may not explain particular variations.(1)

In its broad etymological sense, prejudice—prejudgment—is a term applied to categorical generalizations based on inadequate data and without sufficient regard for individual differences. Such prejudgments are continuously made by everyone on a great variety of subjects. By and large, such generalizations result in some economy of intellectual effort. But inherent in the process of forming prejudgments is the danger of stereotyped thinking. The stereotype is distinguished from the prejudgment only by a greater degree of rigidity. Prejudgment occurs where facts are not available. But stereotype is a process which shows little concern for the facts even when they are available.

Prejudice in its narrowest sense is distinct from prejudgment and stereotypy. It is a sub-category of prejudgment and it uses stereotypy, but is not identical with either. In the psychological context, . . . *prejudice is a pattern of hostility in interpersonal relations which is directed against an entire group, or against its individual members; it fulfills a specific irrational function for its bearer.* This implies that its motivation arises from causes other than the actual qualities of the group against whom the prejudice is directed. If a person alleges that Jews are economically powerful, he is employing stereotyped thinking. He may be right or wrong; if sufficient facts are presented to him, he may change the content of his stereotype to saying: Jews are not powerful economically. But neither of these two statements is in itself a sufficient indication of prejudice. Only when there is evidence that his stereotypes are used as rationalizations for an irrational hostility rooted in his own personality are we talking of prejudice. . . .(2)

S. Andhil Fineberg, a practitioner in the field of intergroup relations for more than twenty-five years, has done much to popularize the findings of psycho-scientific research into prejudice. In his work, *Punishment without Crime,* he defines and illustrates prejudice, introducing a concept that has proved quite novel and thought-provoking. Taking the position that in the interplay of prejudice between the prejudiced person and the object of his bigotry, both are *victims,* he calls the object of such bigotry a *Victimian.* His definition is as follows:

"A Victimian is an individual whose conduct is appraised by others, not only on its intrinsic merit, but also on the fact that he is a member of a certain racial or religious group. In its restricted sense, Victimian means a racial or religious group habitually disesteemed and mistreated because of prejudice. In its widest sense, Victimian means anyone who in a particular situation and even for a moment is wronged because of racial or religious prejudice. . . . The mistreatment and the abuse he suffers result more—and often altogether—from antipathy against his group than from any fault of his own. He is at the receiving end of racial, ethnic or religious hostility." (3)

He moves from the invention of the concept of Victimian to a layman's understanding of prejudice.

Have you heard of the social-distance scale invented by Dr. Emory S. Bogardus? Try it as a test of your own prejudices. Write down on separate lines the names of a dozen or more ethnic and religious groups. After each one write the numerals 1 to 8. Then consider each of those group names. According to your immediate reaction, encircle the numbers that correspond with the eight degrees of social acceptance listed below:

1. *I would exclude them from my country.*
2. *I would admit them to my country but only as visitors.*
3. *I would admit them to citizenship in my country.*
4. *I would admit them to employment in my country.*

5. *I would admit them as classmates in my school.*
6. *I would admit them as neighbors to my street.*
7. *I would admit them to my club as personal chums.*
8. *I would admit them to kinship by marriage.*

The highest numeral encircled for each group indicates your attitude toward that group. If, for example, you used the name of your own racial or religious group, your score on that line would probably be 8, the highest possible score. You might well rate "Americans" at 8. If you measured your feelings about "American Indians," "American Negroes," or "Chinese-Americans," would you score be equally high? Do you tend toward the lower or higher numbers? The higher your score, the less prejudice you harbor.

Dr. Eugene Hartley used the Bogardus Scale on students in eight colleges. Among forty-nine group designations used by him were "Danirean," "Pirenean," and "Wallonians." None of the students ever met a Danirean, a Pirenean, or a Wallonian. No one ever has. These are names of non-existent people. Yet the students who revealed a great deal of intolerance toward other groups had similar attitudes toward these non-such groups.

Conversely, the students who indicated least intolerance toward genuine groups were not intolerant to these fictitious ones. Dr. Hartley drew the logical conclusion: "The degree of intolerance expressed by individuals is a generalized function of the individual and is not completely determined by the specfic group toward which the attitude is directed." Gardner Murphy believes that "This means that there is really no such thing as anti-Negro prejudice or anti-Semitism—except as an expression of purely negative reality, like a vitamin deficiency. There is an acute absense of something, namely of the normal human interchange of ideas or feelings; there is a system of barriers." Disliking an individual *because of his own traits* is not prejudice. Any normal human being, including the members of his own group, would in all likelihood dislike him because of those objectionable attributes or misdeeds. But aversion to a certain group is racial or religious prejudice. There is a barrier between the prejudiced person and the group—a fence, as it were, with which the prejudiced person walls himself in.

Dr. Hartley's test and other experiments reveal a tendency to dislike, to suspect, and even to fear people whose race, religion, or culture is different from our own. There is always "our kind" and "the other kind." Those who happen to be members of our own groupings (and therefore quite like ourselves in language, customs, mannerisms, and the like) belong to our own *in-group*. All other (in relationship to ourselves) belong to *out-groups*. The innate capacity for disliking out-groups may remain dormant and insignificant. It does serve, however, as the tinder which prejudice sparks into a flame. . . .

Our thinking about groups as such is crude and sloppy. We regard them with an affection or with a dislike which bears little or no relation to real merit or demerit. Someday any intelligent person taking a social-distance test, when asked whether he would admit Chinese to his country (or Catholics, Negroes, Protestants, etc.) will reply, "Some, yes, and some, no, depending upon each individual's character." Similarly the question whether he would be willing to have members of such groups as classmates or as neighbors will bring the answer, "Some, yes, and some, no, depending upon the qualities of the individual." Thus far practically every college student to whom this social-distance test has been given has furnished blanket answers which seem to be based on the shallow presumption that all members of each group deserve to be treated alike regardless of their personal qualities. The answers are doubly absurd because practically all who have been tested in American universities say that they would not accept "Jewish Americans" or "Catholic Americans" or "Negro Americans" or "Mexican Americans" as roommates. All of these are Americans! The way we use group names is in many instances highly confusing. We are all prone to speak of "the—s" when we should say "some—s."

How unwittingly we act under the influence of such stereotypes was demonstrated by the lady in this incident: Victor Chit-ai Hoo, a member of the staff of the United Nations, was invited to a meeting at 610 Fifth Avenue, New York. Dr. Hoo misunderstood the message and arrived at Room 610 of the Waldorf-Astoria Hotel where a woman opened the door, revealing a small hotel bedroom. Dr. Hoo, realizing instantly that he had made an error, started to withdraw but the woman ushered him in. She went to the rear of the room, took a bundle out of a closet, and handed it to Dr. Hoo.

He asked, "What is this, please?"

"Why, the laundry, of course," she replied.

Puzzled for a moment, Dr. Hoo bowed graciously and said, "In your country many Chinese are laundrymen, but not *all* Chinese are laundrymen."

The common practice of discussing each permanent group as though it were a distinct, complete little entity set apart creates endless mischief. By such reasoning millions of people are assumed to be as closely related as if they were members of one family, living in the same house, sharing one another's thoughts and minding one another's business. They are assumed to be fully responsible for one another even though, in reality, none of them is personally acquainted with even one per cent of the others. The fact that members of the group are keen economic competitors and that the groups are split into hostile factions on many questions is completely overlooked. In our thinking about each group, we often ignore the fact that within the group there are different social and cultural levels. We seem to be entirely unaware that there are vast ranges of difference between members of each group. We rely on false and misleading stereotypes. We judge people according to preconceived notions that may fit neatly into cartoons but have no place in a scale of values by which we live.

People do not say, "Oh, you bought a chair? It must be upholstered; chairs are upholstered." Nor would they say, "A dress? It must be cotton; dresses are made of cotton." Sane human beings do not make absurd generalizations about impersonal objects. They make generalizations, to be sure, but not ununreasonable ones. But we *do* make the most outrageous generalizations about groups of people. The merits and demerits of our fellow men, the virtues, vices, and characteristics of groups embracing millions of individuals—are predicated on absurd and unwarranted generalities.

Mr. Brown, an American, had accepted the invitation of an Englishman to dine at a restaurant with five of the Englishman's friends. Seated near by were three men, obviously of Anglo-Saxon stock, who had evidently indulged overmuch in alcohol. Nothing was said about it at Brown's table. Despite the noise from the other table Brown's companions did not raise their voices. Brown was enjoying himself fully.

While dessert was being served, two people walked by, talking more loudly than necessary to hear each other.

"A couple of loud Jews," Brown remarked. "Why can't they behave like other fellows?"

His host smiled pleasantly. "You mean like those three men over there who certainly are not Jews?"

"Oh no," said Brown with irritation, "I mean like the other people here."

"You mean like us at this table?"

"Well, yes, of course," said Brown. "Why can't Jews conduct themselves the way we do?"

"Maybe Jews do," said the host, "if you must generalize. You are the only non-Jew at this table."

We inevitably draw conclusions about whole groups, of

course, and not all of them are counterfeit. Certain things can rightfully be said about the culture, customs, institutions, and modes of living of various racial and religious groups. People do belong to such groups. They are influenced in some ways by their group affiliations. There *are* legitimate generalizations about groups, but to recognize whether any particular one is right or spurious, justified or unjustified, requires considerable thought and information, as well as the ability to weigh many factors in the scale of good judgment.

In Plainfield, New Jersey, a public forum was held in the auditorium of a Protestant church. A prominent author brillianty discussed the need for world organization based on democratic principles. A question period followed, during which the speaker enunciated his views even more persuasively. As the discussion drew to a close, one listener arose. "It's all very well," he said, "for you to talk this way and most of us here certainly agree with you, but what about the Catholics? They won't go along with us or accept these ideas."

"I am a Roman Catholic," replied the speaker, "a devout Catholic. My standing in the church is excellent. I cannot assure you that all Catholics will agree with my views, but neither can you assure me that every Protestant agrees with yours."

Prejudices occasionally arise from personal experiences with members of a certain group. The dislike based on an incident involving one or several members of a group is transferred to millions of members of the group whom one has never met. Here the prejudiced person is deceived by his own "association of ideas." More often, however, a prejudice is not initiated by personal experience. It is imbibed from other prejudiced persons. Many of those most prejudiced against Jews have never met one. Nowhere in the United States are Catholics more disliked than in certain rural areas where there are no Catholics. On practically all tests of opinion among Americans the Turks have received one of the worst ratings, despite the fact that most Americans have never met a Turk and know practically nothing about Turks. The mere fact that the term "the terrible Turk" has been coined and sticks so readily in the human mind may be largely responsible for this unjustified aversion.

Some prejudices are based on historical antagonisms passed on and preserved through generations, even for many centuries. There is the story of two little children, Herman and Edith Cohen, who had associated with their Christian neighbors on the best of terms until one Sunday afternoon when they met with sudden hostility. As they approached some of the other children they were rebuffed.

"You can't play with us any more," they were told bluntly.

"Why not?" they asked in bewilderment.

"Because we learned in Sunday-school this morning that you Jews killed Jesus."

The Cohen children were appalled. They conferred for several minutes, unable to find any explanation of what had occurred. They were sure no member of their family had committed such a crime. Finally they hit upon an answer as good as any which might occur to youngsters who had never before heard this accusation. Herman approached the others and offered what he considered a plausible explanation.

"Please," he pleaded, "we didn't kill Jesus. It must have been some other Jewish children. Maybe it was the family next door."

A more informed person could have replied that crucifixion was a Roman form of execution and was never employed by Jews. But aside from details of fact one does wonder why the crucifixion story is taught by some Christian educators in a manner that stigmatizes people of today for a tragedy of nineteen centuries ago.

To trace the origins of every extraordinary bit of racial and religious prejudice would take us far afield. In one instance it may have had its roots in a mother's attempts to obtain obedience by frightening a child with "the Chinese bogeyman." In another it may have been an inferiority complex seeking compensation. It may have been the sneering tone with which parents spoke the name of a group, or something read in a storybook. Discovering how individuals absorb their various prejudices is an intricate job for psychologists. The sources of the infection are so deeply hidden that rarely can an adult recall the moment when he first acquired an aversion towards a certain group.

Once a prejudiced opinion is adopted by an individual, the prejudice perpetuates itself, binding the bigot to everything that might weaken his prejudice and steering his attention to everything that strengthens it. A prejudiced man overlooks or ascribes to *human* conduct the misdeeds of members of his own group. Anything *praiseworthy* done by a member of the disliked group is considered the act of that *individual.* As soon, however, as something objectionable about a member of the condemned group comes to his attention, the prejudiced person extends the blame to *all* members of that group and becomes the more intolerant.

That prejudgments about groups can be more potent than reality itself is demonstrated by "serial reproduction" through such experiments as the following:

A large placard is set up in the front of a room—in this instance a drawing of a subway station, where one man is sprawled on a bench and another is reading a newspaper. The most prominent figure is a white man who holds an old-fashioned straight razor with the blade open. A Negro is also prominent in the picture. His hands are empty. The audience studies the card until they know what is on it, then the placard is put out of sight. Five or six persons who have not seen the drawing are called in, one at a time. The first to enter is told accurately what was on the card. He tells it to the second; the second to the third; the third to the fourth; and so on. Inevitably one of the five or six who has not seen the picture informs the next person that the Negro is holding the open razor. Though some details fade out, in all of the subsequent retellings the Negro with the razor remains, despite the fact that in the picture *the white man* held the razor. The actual picture evaporates and the groundless idea that a Negro is more likely to hold an open razor than a white man prevails.

A Turkish gentleman was brought to a social gathering and introduced to an elderly woman.

"They tell me you are a Turk," said the matron.

"I am," replied the Turkish citizen.

"Where's your fez?" asked the lady.

"I don't wear a fez," was the reply.

Thereupon she smiled knowingly. "You can't fool me into believing you're a Turk. You're not a Turk or you'd wear a fez."

The dictionary definition of a "fez" is "a form of felt or cloth cap, usually red and having a tassel, *formerly* worn as the national headdress of the Turks." But to one who learned in childhood that Turks wear fezzes, and who is impervious to facts, the fez remains the one essential feature of Turkish identity. Similarly when prejudiced persons meet members of some group who have none of the objectionable characteristics alleged about their group, the reaction of the prejudiced is, "You're not typical of the group. You're an exception." The hard core of prejudice remains despite the very best evidence that it is unjustified.

Prejudice makes people unwilling to meet Victimians socially, much as a preconceived dislike of Limburger cheese will keep one from tasting it. The prejudiced not only think they know all the pertinent facts but are also determined that nothing shall change their impressions. They are like the fellow who said, "I am glad that I dislike cabbage, because if I didn't dislike it I would eat cabbage and might even enjoy eating it. And it would certainly be awful for me to eat it because I hate it like poison."

The tenacious grip of prejudice on the minds and hearts of men is indicated by even the brief diagnosis we have made of its relation to the individual. But the social aspects of prejudice and its offshoot, discrimination, offer even more startling proof of the virulence and endurance of this mental blight. The very root questions that plague every practical and forward-looking person—How shall we keep children free of prejudice when their parents instill their own intolerant attitudes? How shall we teach youngsters to eschew prejudice when their teachers are often not free of prejudice? How shall we prevent the new generation from becoming infected by their environment?—these and scores of similar questions imply a tacit recognition that society itself is a breeding ground for the contagion.

When prejudice against an out-group has once rooted itself in the life of a community, social pressures make it increasingly difficult to resist it. These pressures are sometimes the most direct and primitive—hard demands, dire threats, and brutal physical violence. A sheriff in a town in an infected area, when asked why it was impossible to persuade witnesses at a lynching to testify against the perpetrators, replied, "Because they know that anybody who takes part in a lynching would also kill an informer."

Usually, however, it is not necessary to resort to violence to force acceptance of the attitudes of a dominant in-group. The threat, even the implied threat, of excluding non-conformists from a part in community life is usually sufficient to enforce at least a passive acquiescence. Even when the prejudiced group is not numerically superior, there are often effective ways of forcing the more tolerant majority to bow to their demands. In effect, the prejudiced assert their position by saying, "Either you will respect our convictions, or we'll break up the game." The threat of non-co-operation or outright hostilities frequently preserves the remnants of prejudice against the will of the majority.

A city official was inviting seven men to discuss a certain civic project at lunch. The third man he called, a Mr. Dwight, asked who would be present. The commissioner gave the names of the six others he had in mind. One of them, Lucas, was a Victimian.

"I've never eaten at the same table with one of Lucas' people," said Dwight, "and I don't intend to."

"But Lucas is a splendid person," the commissioner protested.

"Surely you have no objection to him personally."

"He's all right, but I'm not eating with him. Just count me out of this."

Recalling the incident later, the commissioner said, "If I had already called Lucas I would have stuck to my guns and left Dwight out. But I had not yet phoned Lucas, and Dwight was in a position to do much more for the project than Lucas could. I pleaded with Dwight to change his mind, but to no avail. Finally I yielded. All except Dwight would have been happy to dine with Lucas. But what happened? Five of us were outvoted, as it were, by one prejudiced person."

Kurt Lewin, who made brilliant contributions to the study of human relationships, found that "many stereotypes and dislikes are anchored not so much in the individual's personality as in groups to which the individual belongs." Because his group has acquired a relatively superior position, the individual may find it possible to disesteem or mistreat another group. These social divisions often have their origins in historical processes. In some instances it was conquest which produced dominance in one group and subservience in another. American Indians were the victims of conquest and American Negroes, too, since slavery was a form of conquest. Time of migration, economic position, and dozens of other factors have likewise created and perpetuated group inequalities on American soil.

Control of the social mechanisms makes it possible for the dominant group to stamp the disadvantaged group as inferior. The suppressed are relegated to "their place" in the social order and are said to be happiest "in their own place"—a very lowly place where humiliation, squalor, and ignorance are ostensibly the handmaidens of happiness. Adverse generalizations strengthen the impression that all of the members of a disadvantaged racial or religious group have the same objectionable traits. They are pictured as lazy, selfish, slovenly, impoverished, cowardly, rude, boisterous, avaricious, drunken, dishonest, hideous, cruel, murderous, moronic, or otherwise obnoxious. Since they are presumably so base and so inferior they ought not to expect to be treated on a plane of parity with the "superior group."

The elaboration and preservation of this fraud are readily accomplished because the channels of communication are largely controlled by members of the prestige group. Literature, art, and other media of expression are dominated by them. Laws, social customs, and community mores are determined to a great extent by those who have initial economic and political dominance. In all of these media the counterfeit concepts which differentiate the "superior" from the "inferior" groups are—by usage and reiteration—inculcated as self-evident truths.

In a thoroughly democratic society group inequalities would be unthinkable. But they do exist and make their deep impress upon us, upon our fellow Americans, and upon the world. In ten thousand subtle ways we are guided into the belief that there is a prestige group, socially superior and far more admirable than the others. By birth, faith, or color half the people of the United States cannot belong to the "superior" class.(4)

That group conflict can be "conditioned" has been established in the course of experiments with youngsters in which, even where completely homogeneous groups were involved, artificial distinctions were created and dramatized with the result that group conflict was created. The experiments then called for a process of "de-conditioning," designed to throw light on the techniques best suited to deal with conflict situations. Contrary to the hypothesis of many layman and workers alike in the field of intergroup relations, mere social contact between groups not only failed to lessen tension, but often increased it. On the other hand, cooperative efforts to meet an emergency or situation which threatened rival groups jointly had a marked effect in reducing both group and individual hostility.

In "Experiments in Group Conflict," an article which appeared in Scientific American (November, 1956), Dr. Muzafer Sherif describes the results of "controlled situation" experiments in boys' summer camps in the 1949-1954 period.

Conflict between groups—whether between boys' gangs, social classes, "races" or nations—has no simple cause, nor is mankind yet in sight of a cure. It is often rooted deep in personal, social, economic, religious and historical forces. Nevertheless it is possible to identify certain general factors which have a crucial influence on the attitude of any group toward others. Social scientists have long sought to bring these factors to light by studying what might be called the "natural history" of groups and group relations. Intergroup conflict and harmony is not a subject that lends itself easily to laboratory experiments. But in recent years there has been a beginning of attempts to investigate the problem under controlled yet lifelike conditions, and I shall report here the results of a program of experimental studies of groups which I started in 1948. . . .

We wanted to conduct our study with groups of the informal type, where group organization and attitudes would evolve naturally and spontaneously, without formal direction or external pressures. For this purpose we conceived that an isolated summer camp would make a good experimental setting, and that decision led us to choose as subjects boys about 11 or 12 years old, who would find camping natural and fascinating. Since our aim was to study the development of group relations among these boys under carefully controlled conditions, with as little interference as possible from personal neuroses, background influences or prior experiences, we selected normal boys of homogeneous background who did not know one another before they came to the camp.

They were picked by a long and thorough procedure. We interviewed each boy's family, teachers and school officials, studied his school and medical records, obtained his scores on personality tests and observed him in his classes and at play with his schoolmates. With all this information we were able to assure ourselves that the boys chosen were of like kind and background: all were healthy, socially well-adjusted, somewhat above average in intelligence and from stable, white, Protestant, middle class homes.

None of the boys was aware that he was part of an experiment on group relations. The investigators appeared as a regular camp staff—camp directors, counselors and so on. The boys met one another for the first time in buses that took them to the camp, and so far as they knew it was a normal summer of camping. To keep the situation as lifelike as possible, we conducted all our experiments within the framework of regular camp activities and games. We set up projects which were so interesting and attractive that the boys plunged into them enthusiastically without suspecting that they might be test situations. Unobtrusively we made records of their behavior, even using "candid" cameras and microphones when feasible.

We began by observing how the boys became a coherent group. The first of our camps was conducted in the hills of northern Connecticut in the summer of 1949. When the boys arrived, they were all housed at first in one large bunkhouse. As was to be expected, they quickly formed particular friendships and chose buddies. We had deliberately put all the boys together in this expectation, because we wanted to see what would happen later after the boys were separated into different groups. Our object was to reduce the factor of personal attraction in the formation of groups. In a few days we divided the boys into two groups and put them in different cabins. Before doing so, we asked each boy informally who his best friends were, and then took pains to place the "best friends" in different groups so far as possible. (The pain of separation was assuaged by allowing each group to go at once on a hike and camp-out.)

As everyone knows, a group of strangers brought together in some common activity soon acquires an informal and spontaneous kind of organization. It comes to look upon some members as leaders, divides up duties, adopts unwritten norms of behavior, develops an *esprit de corps*. Our boys followed this pattern as they shared a series of experiences. In each group the boys pooled their efforts, organized duties and divided up tasks in work and play. Different individuals assumed different responsibilities. One boy excelled in cooking. Another led in athletics. Others, though not outstanding in any one skill, could be counted on to pitch in and do their level best in anything the group attempted. One or two seemed to disrupt activities, to start teasing at the wrong moment or offer useless suggestions. A few boys consistently had good suggestions and showed ability to coordinate the efforts of others in carrying them through. Within a few days one person had proved himself more resourceful and skillful than the rest. Thus, rather quickly, a leader and lieutenants emerged. Some boys sifted toward the bottom of the heap, while others jockeyed for higher positions.

We watched these developments closely and rated the boys' relative positions in the group, not only on the basis of our own observations but also by informal sounding of the boys' opinions as to who got things started, who got things done, who could be counted on to support group activities.

As the group became an organization, the boys coined nicknames. The big, blond, hardy leader of one group was dubbed "Baby Face" by his admiring followers. A boy with a rather long head became "Lemon Head." Each group developed its own jargon, special jokes, secrets and special ways of performing tasks. One group, after killing a snake near a place where it had gone to swim, named the place "Moccasin Creek" and thereafter preferred this swimming hole to any other, though there were better ones nearby.

Wayward members who failed to do things "right" or who did not contribute their bit to the common effort found themselves receiving the "silent treatment," ridicule or even threats. Each group selected symbols and a name, and they had these put on their caps and T-shirts. The 1954 camp was conducted in Oklahoma, near a famous hideaway of Jesse James called Robber's Cove. The two groups of boys at this camp named themselves the Rattlers and the Eagles.

Our conclusions on every phase of the study were based on a variety of observations, rather than on any single method. For example, we devised a game to test the boys' evaluations of one another. Before an important baseball game, we set up a target board for the boys to throw at, on the pretense of making practice for the game more interesting. There were no marks on the front of the board for the boys to judge objectively how close the ball came to a bull's-eye, but, unknown to them, the board was wired to flashing lights behind so that an observer could see exactly where the ball hit. We found that the boys consistently overestimated the performances by the most highly regarded members of their group and underestimated the scores of those of low social standing.

The attitudes of group members were even more dramatically illustrated during a cook-out in the woods. The staff supplied the boys with unprepared food and let them cook it themselves. One boy promptly started to build a fire, asking for help in getting wood. Another attacked the raw hamburger to make patties. Others prepared a place to put buns, relishes and the like. Two mixed soft drinks from flavoring and sugar. One boy who stood around without helping was told by the others to "get to it." Shortly the fire was blazing and the cook had hamburgers sizzling. Two boys distributed them as rapidly as they became edible. Soon it was time for the watermelon. A low-ranking member of the group took a knife and started toward the melon. Some of the boys protested. The most highly regarded boy in the group took over the knife, saying, "You guys who yell the loudest get yours last."

When the two groups in the camp had developed group organization and spirit, we proceeded to the experimental studies of intergroup relations. The groups had had no previous encounters; indeed, in the 1954 camp at Robber's Cove the two groups came in separate buses and were kept apart while each acquired a group feeling.

Our working hypothesis was that when two groups have conflicting aims—*i.e.*, when one can achieve its ends only at the expense of the other—their members will become hostile to each other even though the groups are composed of normal well-adjusted individuals. There is a corollary to this assumption which we shall consider later. To produce friction between the groups of boys we arranged a tournament of games: baseball, touch football, a tug-of-war, a treasure hunt and so on. The tournament started in a spirit of good sportsmanship. But as it progressed good feeling soon evaporated. The members of each group began to call their rivals "stinkers," "sneaks" and "cheaters." They refused to have anything more to do with individuals in the opposing group. The boys in the 1949 camp turned against buddies whom they had chosen as "best friends" when they first arrived at the camp. A large proportion of the boys in each group gave negative ratings to all the boys in the other. The rival groups made threatening posters and planned raids, collecting secret hoards of green apples for ammunition. In the Robber's Cave camp the Eagles, after a defeat in a tournament game, burned a banner left behind by the Rattlers;

the next morning the Rattlers seized the Eagles' flag when they arrived on the athletic field. From that time on name-calling, scuffles and raids were the rule of the day.

Within each group, of course, solidarity increased. There were changes: one group deposed its leader because he could not "take it" in the contests with the adversary; another group overnight made something of a hero of a big boy who had previously been regarded as a bully. But morale and cooperativeness within the group became stronger. It is noteworthy that this heightening of cooperativeness and generally democratic behavior did not carry over to the group's relations with other groups.

We now turned to the other side of the problem: How can two groups in conflict be brought into harmony? We first undertook to test the theory that pleasant social contacts between members of conflicting groups will reduce friction between them. In the 1954 camp we brought the hostile Rattlers and Eagles together for social events: going to the movies, eating in the same dining room and so on. But far from reducing conflict, these situations only served as opportunities for the rival groups to berate and attack each other. In the dining-hall line they shoved each other aside, and the group that lost the contest for the head of the line shouted "Ladies first!" at the winner. They threw paper, food and vile names at each other at the tables. An Eagle bumped by a Rattler was admonished by his fellow Eagles to brush "the dirt" off his clothes.

We then returned to the corollary of our assumption about the creation of conflict. Just as competition generates friction, working in a common endeavor should promote harmony. It seemed to us, considering group relations in the everyday world, that where harmony between groups is established, the most decisive factor is the existence of "super-ordinate" goals which have a compelling appeal for both but which neither could achieve without the other. To test this hypothesis experimentally, we created a series of urgent, and natural, situations which challenged our boys.

One was a breakdown in the water supply. Water came to our camp in pipes from a tank about a mile away. We arranged to interrupt it and then called the boys together to inform them of the crisis. Both groups promptly volunteered to search the water line for the trouble. They worked together harmoniously, and before the end of the afternoon they had located and corrected the difficulty.

A similar opportunity offered itself when the boys requested a movie. We told them that the camp could not afford to rent one.

The two groups then got together, figured out how much each group would have to contribute, chose the film by a vote and enjoyed the showing together.

One day the two groups went on an outing at a lake some distance away. A large truck was to go to town for food. But when everyone was hungry and ready to eat, it developed that the truck would not start (we had taken care of that). The boys got a rope—the same rope they had used in their acrimonious tug-of-war—and all pulled together to start the truck.

These joint efforts did not immediately dispel hostility. At first the groups returned to the old bickering and name-calling as soon as the job in hand was finished. But gradually the series of cooperative acts reduced friction and conflict. The members of the two groups began to feel more friendly to each other. For example, a Rattler whom the Eagles disliked for his sharp tongue and skill in defeating them became a "good egg." The boys stopped shoving in the meal line. They no longer called each other names, and sat together at the table. New friendships developed between individuals in the two groups.

In the end the groups were actively seeking opportunities to mingle, to entertain and "treat" each other. They decided to hold a joint campfire. They took turns presenting skits and songs. Members of both groups requested that they go home together on the same bus, rather than on the separate buses in which they had come. On the way the bus stopped for refreshments. One group still had five dollars which they had won as a prize in a contest. They decided to spend this sum on refreshments. On their own initiative they invited their former rivals to be their guests for malted milks.

Our interviews with the boys confirmed this change. From choosing their "best friends" almost exclusively in their own group, many of them shifted to listing boys in the other group as best friends. They were glad to have a second chance to rate boys in the other group, some of them remarking that they had changed their minds since the first rating made after the tournament. Indeed they had. The new ratings were largely favorable.

Efforts to reduce friction and prejudice between groups in our society have usually followed rather different methods. Much attention has been given to bringing members of hostile groups together socially, to communicating accurate and favorable information about one group to the other, and to bringing the leaders of groups together to enlist their influence. But as everyone knows, such measures sometimes reduce intergroup tensions and sometimes do not. Social contacts, as our experiments demonstrated, may only serve as occasions for intensifying conflict. Favorable information about a disliked group may be ignored or reinterpreted to fit stereotyped notions about the group. Leaders cannot act without regard for the prevailing temper in their own groups.

What our limited experiments have shown is that the possibilities for achieving harmony are greatly enhanced when groups are brought together to work toward common ends. Then favorable information about a disliked group is seen in a new light, and leaders are in a position to take bolder steps toward cooperation. In short, hostility gives way when groups pull together to achieve overriding goals which are real and compelling to all concerned. (5)

We have thus far considered prejudice from a definitional point of view. What is the process by which this static mechanism is triggered? Prejudiced behavior in individuals is often traceable to their emotional makeup, or more accurately, their emotional deficiencies. Cumulatively, this results in a floating malaise which, when crystallized on a given issue desegregation, for example—expresses itself in articulate and often virulent hostility. The fixation process is stimulated by agitators, persons who for personal gain, ego satisfaction or sheer fanaticism, are the catalysts of overt prejudice. The dynamics of prejudice may be said, therefore, to consist of the following elements: 1) stereotyped thinking as an element in intergroup relations; 2) individual anxiety and frustration which seeks emotional satisfaction in prejudice; 3) the cumulative impact of the anxiety-prejudice pattern, resulting in a general social malaise of anxiety and insecurity and "floating prejudice;" 4) the existence of a major social issue or event which crystallizes both the malaise and the prejudice reaction; 5) the catalyst of the agitator.

For a precise analysis of these several elements, we turn again to the materials developed in the Studies in Prejudice. The excerpt which follows is from the previously noted *Anti-Semitism and Emotional Disorder*. Those which follow are from *Prophets of Deceit* by Leo Lowenthal and Norbert Guterman.

Emotional Predispositions to Prejudice

ANXIETY: As is characteristic of analytic patients, all the individuals included in this study suffered from anxiety. In most instances, however, a large component of the anxiety was of a special nature: it was diffuse, pervasive, relatively unorganized, and not adequately channelized through specific symptomformation. Generally it was not experienced as a conscious dread but manifested itself indirectly in various forms of social discomfort and disability.

Socially, economically, emotionally, and sexually, they are plagued by an exaggerated sense of vulnerability. Often, these fears are not apparent on the surface, but analysis reveals their existence under a façade of superficial self-confidence. The general picture is one of weakness and incompleteness in total personality organization, and fear of injury in a vast variety of social contexts. Because of their inner weakness and neglible insight, these patients view the outer world as hostile, evil, and inexplicably hard. They fail to see any relation between their own personalities and whatever difficulties they experience. This is, of course the result of projection.

Authors of detective stories and murder mysteries know as well as psychiatrists that nothing is more terrifying than the *unknown* danger. When the dark and uncanny enemy becomes identified and can then be labeled, tension subsides even though the real danger may still exist in a quite different direction. It will be well to remember this in order to understand why people who suffer from such pervasive, diffuse anxiety cling tenaciously and irrationally to their anti-Semitism, once they have mistakenly come to regard the Jews as the cause of the evil. Unfortunately for them, notwithstanding this specious identification of the "enemy," the anxiety persists.

CONFUSION OF THE CONCEPT OF SELF: Plagued by a vague apprehension of the world at large, these patients seem to derive little, if any, strength from their own personal identity. So confused and vague is their self-image that they do not seem to know who or what they are, what they desire, and what they can forego. This confusion carries over directly to the roles they play in life. With little regard for facts and the external situation of their lives they waver between feelings of inferiority and superiority; between regarding themselves as strong or weak, and between considering themselves as members of this or that group, or as completely isolated human beings. In some cases they do not even waver between extremes; they simply fail entirely to organize their psychological identity. . . .

These patients do not seem to have achieved a clear separation of their individual selves from the surrounding world. Unable to define clearly their individuality or at least to recognize themselves as comparatively stable entities, they attempt to achieve stability by utilizing props selected from the external situation. When they resort to one after another of a series of such props without effecting relief of emotional tension, doubts about the identity of the self become painfully and plainly exposed. . . .

These feelings of inner doubt and ambivalence toward one's own self are frequently too painful to be accepted without compensatory efforts. Inferiority, weakness, dependency, a tendency toward compulsive submissiveness and basic passivity, are often concealed from the world and even from one's own consciousness. The apparent substitute for such awareness is a tendency toward compensatory self-aggrandizement. . . .

Whatever the manifestation, however, such persons are particularly sensitive to the possession by anyone else of an unequivocal identity. Organized anti-Semitism, for example, has always shown an irrational concern for establishing Jewish identity. The Nazi regime, to achieve this end, employed the yellow stripe, the investigation of "Jewish blood" as far back as three generations, and the formulation of pseudoscientific racial mythology in which a "Jewish race" could be labeled. The same irrational concern with Jewish identity is displayed by the American anti-Semite, who as likely as not, will claim the ability to identify a Jew by looking at him. One patient, a commuter, whiled away the time during his regular train trips by "smelling out" Jews, and he reported greater success in this venture during the summer months. . . .

INTERPERSONAL RELATIONS: Because the self-image is unstable and confused, it is extremely difficult for these anti-Semitic personalities to achieve satisfactory interpersonal relationships. At best their capacities permit them to establish little more than immature and incomplete human relationships. Such precarious relationships are continuously endangered by attitudes of over-aggressiveness or overdependence, both of which serve to estrange the other person. What is worse, often there is not even the capacity for such tentative, incomplete relationships, since fear and mistrust of other people make some of these patients uneasy, shy, and awkward in company. Quite a few have never known a relationship deeper than that of casual acquaintance. . . . Others have a more successful mechanism for disguising their incapacity to establish genuine relationships. But at best such disguises deceive the outer world and sometimes the self; they never lead to the establishment of warm, human relations. . . .The admission of such resignation is rare. Generally the patients make frantic efforts to establish human contacts, but their deep-rooted doubts about themselves frustrate their attempts even before they get started. Unwittingly they destroy every incipient relationship by wavering between extremes of behavior. . . . Shifts between ingratiating and aggressive behavior, shifts which are hardly related to the real situation but are produced mainly as a result of deep-lying insecurity and emotional confusion, lead to repeated failures in social and personal contacts. The result of such failure is increased emotional isolation.

CONFORMITY AND THE FEAR OF THE DIFFERENT: The absence of warm human relationships causes these patients shame and suffering. Consequently, what they cannot achieve within themselves they pretend to achieve on the social level by putting up a "good front" of sociability. . . .

In most cases the strong emphasis on conformity to group standards is basically shallow. . . . Ordinarily, this type of person seeks to reap the rewards of social conformity, but unconsciously his fear of submission is too great. His striving for acceptance is governed by the desire to appear like everyone else rather than to achieve genuine identification, and frequently he shifts from one group to another, over-protesting the strength of his allegiance to this or that cause according to the immediate situation.

To the person beset by such a conflict concerning group adherence, those people who are supposedly "different," and who in addition do not seem to wish to abandon their difference, are an eternal source of provocation. The Jews appear to the anti-Semite as different from himself, and yet they appear to be alike among themselves. Hence qualities of uncanniness are attributed to Jews. On the one hand they seem to have the courage to be different; on the other, they seem also to succeed in being identified within a group. The very existence of the Jews, then, is a constant and painful reminder of the anti-Semite's own emotional deficiencies.

That is why the fear of the "different" is not in proportion to the extent of the objective, measurable difference. Rather it is in proportion to the emotional deficiency which produces the need for conformity and belonging. The "difference," as a result, is subjectively translated into an attack on group identity; the "difference" is consequently exaggerated, and the fear increases.

Those anti-Semites who habitually assert that "some of my best friends are Jews" demonstrate their intolerance and extraordinary sensitiveness to "difference" by this transparent denial of hostility. The actual difference does not register with them; it never crosses the threshold of their perception. They determine what Jewishness means according to their own arbitrary standard. Such a Jewish friend may be Jewish looking or non-Jewish looking, rich or poor, a native American or foreign-born, an assimilated or a non-assimilated Jew, and so on. These dichotomies can, of course, be combined in all variations, and produce different external stimuli. But, again, the reaction to "difference" is not in proportion to actual measurable degrees of difference, but rather to the implied threat to self-esteem contained in *any* difference.

All prejudiced persons insist on conformity within their own group to the extent of trying to destroy the nonconformist. The "difference" of their outsider, on the other hand, has a special significance; it is exaggerated because it serves a specific psychological function. By emphasizing this "difference," the prejudiced person achieves, at least negatively, a sense of identification with his own group. By conforming to Group A, he gets at least the false security of feeling that he is not a member of the supposedly inferior Group B. Within his own ranks, however, to assert difference is hazardous. This insistence on conformity in one's own group is paired, on a deeper level, with an unconscious wish to rebel against one's own group.

Since conformity connotes surrender of individuality, a person who represents "difference," even though passively, symbolizes strength, maturity, independence, superiority, and the ability to stand up against others unashamed of his own "difference." Such a person immediately looms as dangerous. He must not be tolerated in the ranks of the "ordinary" people but must be made an outsider. For the prejudiced person cannot bear the implied comparison. Because of the inherent weakness of his own self-image, the "different" person represents a potential menace to his own integrity—or whatever there is left of it— as an individual. The inevitable response is to attack the menace, the person who symbolizes difference.

"If only the Jews behaved like everybody else!" This frequent statement of the apparently reasonable anti-Semite, with its emphasis on conformity rather than on inherent merits or deficiencies of behavior, is an unconscious betrayal of what is wrong in himself.

REALITY ADAPTATION: The emotional deficiencies of these patients, extending beyond the sphere of human relations, seem also to have impaired their capacity to establish a satisfactory relationship with external objects. Their very perception of reality is vague, dull, and indefinitely formed. Since there is nothing that interests them for its own sake, they rarely know what to do with themselves in their spare time. Drabness permeates their entire emotional adaptation to reality. Their affective responses seem shallow and colorless, and quite often restricted. In the analytic situation, however, they occasionally become imaginatively affective when they are dominated by the urge to restructure reality in accordance with their unconscious needs; such affective excitements often color the expression of their anti-Semitism. When it seems to them that they have discovered the Jew as the source of all evil, they resemble schizophrenics who have suddenly seen the light. In such futile attempts to restructure reality, they approach a state that is not so much neurotic as psychotic. And yet so thoroughly imbued by drabness are some of these patients that they cannot produce the semblance of strong affects even against the Jew.

Apart from such outlets as anti-Semitism provides, this lusterless quality prevails generally in such patients. It is not surprising that no evidence of clearly defined life-goals can be found in these persons. Unaware of what they want, they seem vaguely concerned with impotent desires to establish their relationship to the outside world.

The selective perception of reality, described earlier, is thus matched by a selective adaptation to it. Although the break with reality is never complete, the rift is deep; so deep that such persons can hardly escape awareness of its existence. From this stems the frantic attempt to restore spontaneous contact with the real world. Anti-Semitic attitudes, however futile, signify one of these disguised attempts.

CONSCIENCE DEVELOPMENT AND REPRESSION: One further facet of the reaction pattern which characterizes these prejudiced persons is the quality of their conscience. Generally speaking, there is little evidence of a consistent value system protected by a well-developed conscience. Genuine guilt feelings are sometimes entirely absent. Most specifically, most of the patients do not appear to have overt guilt feelings about their anti-Semitism. (An interesting exception occurs, however, with that small number of persons who are committed to an ideology of political liberalism. These people do feel ashamed of their anti-Semitism.)

Even apart from their absent or deficient sence of guilt about their anti-Semitism, the political "liberals" and other anti-Semites provide ample evidence of an insufficient conscience development. Often not even the most elementary standards of decency are maintained, as abundant examples make clear. There is the wealthy businessman who cheats his newspaper dealer out of small change; the father who happily eats the candies which have been entrusted to him for his children; the mother who leaves her small child alone at home because she feels like going for a walk. One patient, with great delight, reported to his analyst a fantasy, stimulated by his wife's slight indisposition, in which he imagined that she would die, and that he would then be able to sell her recently purchased mink coat. The price of fur coats having risen, he reveled in the idea of the profit he could make in this manner.

In other cases, there is a definite guilt reaction which may perhaps be substantial in intensity, but which is unreliable and fickle in kind. This type of guilt reaction is often treacherous in interpersonal relations. In such cases, people tend to equate the Jews with their own conscience to whatever extent it has been developed, only to reject both. This is most clearly expressed in the woman patient, who sadly neglected her child. She had a great deal of personal contact with both Jews and Irish. "The Irish," she said, "want me to play and enjoy myself. The Jews want me to work, to be serious and punctual." Actually, in her way of life she followed the "Irish" (or what she believed to be "Irish") rather than the ways of the "Jews." This woman had a conscience, but it failed to operate in the discharge of her maternal responsibilities. . . .

Psychoanalytic theory suggests that in such patients the process of *repression* in some measure fails—a trend that seems to be borne out by the evidence of our case studies. The effort to prevent a particular impulse from entering consciousness is never sufficiently strong or consistent. Hence the frequent changes in manifest behavior between attempts to be ingratiating—a temporary repression—and overt hostility—the breaking through of the repressed.

The effort involved in these frequent shifts, together with the difficulties created in human relationships by such unreliable and unpredictable responses, imposes considerable strain. Nothing is more understandable than the relief that such persons experience when they are under no social compulsion to repress hostility. Perhaps this is what occurs in some subcultures in the United States where anti-Semitism meets with no disapproval. Since the effort of repression is not required, there is no pain experienced in the failure to repress. In these instances, externalized and pseudo-objectively justified anti-Semitism serves as a safety valve—here one can let oneself go without getting into inner conflict.

Thus far we have described some of the emotional predispositions common to all of our cases. Each of these individuals is plagued by pervasive anxiety. Deeply confused in his own self-image, he derives no strength from his personal identity with which to face a menacing world. His personal relationships are shallow and unsatisfying. His group relations are characterized by an exaggerated surface conformity, beneath which lurks a primitive, untamed hostility. Within his group the slightest indication of nonconformity appears as a threat. Outside his group, differences are exaggerated. Lacking a basis of genuine identification, he tends in a compensatory way to define his group status by reference to qualities de does not actually possess. He achieves only a partial adaptation to reality, and is unable to develop spontaneous and genuine personal relationships. His conscience is underdeveloped and unreliable, his repressions incomplete and inefficient, thereby necessitating recourse to the laborious tasks of conscious suppression.

In the foregoing description of the emotional factors which predispose the individual toward anti-Semitism, it has often been necessary to isolate emotional tendencies for the purpose of systematic presentation. It is self-evident, however, that they do not exist as isolated traits at all, but are dynamically interrelated within the personality.(6)

In *Prophets of Deceit,* the emotional predispositions outlined above are related to the specific emotions on which the agitator seeks to play in building his following, while at the same time capitalizing on the malaise through which individual anxieties, insecurities and protests can be translated into a mass movement.

. . . the grievances the agitator voices do not refer to any clearly delineated material or moral condition. The only constant elements discernible in this mass of grievances are references to certain emotions or emotional complexes. These may be roughly divided as follows:

Distrust: The agitator plays on his audience's suspicions of all social phenomena impinging on its life in ways it does not understand. Foreign refugees cash in on the "gullibility" of Americans, whom he warns not to be "duped" by internationalists. Strewn through the output of the agitator are such words as *hoax, corrupt, insincere, duped, manipulate.*

Dependence: The agitator seems to assume that he is addressing people who suffer from a sense of helplessness and passivity. He plays on the ambivalent nature of this complex which on the one hand reflects a protest against manipulation and on the other hand a wish to be protected, to belong to a strong organization or be led by a strong leader.

Exclusion: The agitator suggests that there is an abundance of material and spiritual goods, but that the people do not get what they are entitled to. The American taxpayer's money is used to help everyone but himself—"we feed foreigners," the agitator complains, while we neglect our own millions of unemployed.

Anxiety: This complex manifests itself in a general premonition of disaster to come, a prominent part of which seems to be the middle-class fear of a dislocation of its life by revolutionary action, and its suspicion that the moral mainstays of social life are being undermined. The agitator speaks of "the darkest hour in American history" and graphically describes a pervasive sense of fear and insecurity. . . .

Disillusionment: This complex is seen in such remarks as the agitator's characterization of politics as "make-believe, pretense, pretext, sham, fraud, deception, dishonesty, falsehood, hypocrisy. . . ." In fact, "whenever a legislative body meets, liberties of the people are endangered by subtle and active interests." Ideological slogans inspire resentment, "Democracy A Misnomer, A Trick Word Used by Jew and Communistic Internationalists to Confuse and Befuddle American Citizens. . . ." Values and ideals are enemy weapons, covering up the machinations of sinister powers which, "taking advantage of the mass ignorance of our people, accomplish their purposes under the cloak of humanitarianism and justice."

. . . are these merely fleeting, insubstantial, purely accidental and personal emotions blown up by the agitator into genuine complaints or are they themselves a constant rooted in the social structure? The answer seems unavoidable: these feelings cannot be dismissed as either accidental or imposed, they are basic to modern society. Distrust, dependance, exclusion, anxiety, and disillusionment blend together to form a fundamental condition of modern life: *malaise. . . .*

On the plane of immediate awareness, the malaise seems to originate in the individual's own depths and is experienced by him as an apparently isolated and purely psychic or spiritual crisis. It enhances his sense of antagonism to the rest of the world. These groups in our society that are at present most susceptible to agitation seem to experience this malaise with particular acuteness—perhaps precisely because they do not confront social coercion in its more direct forms.

Although malaise actually reflects social reality, it also veils and distorts it. Malaise is neither an illusion of the audience nor a mere imposition by the agitator; it is a psychological symptom of an oppressive situation. The agitator does not try to diagnose the relationship of this symptom to the underlying social situation. Instead he tricks his audience into accepting the very situation that produced its malaise. Under the guise of protest against the oppressive situation, the agitator binds his audience to it. Since this pseudo-protest never produces a genuine solution, it merely leads the audience to seek permanent relief from a permanent predicament by means of irrational outbursts. The agitator does not create the malaise, but he aggravates and fixates it because he bars the path to overcoming it.

Those afflicted by the malaise ascribe social evil not to an unjust or obsolete form of society or to a poor organization of an adequate society, but rather to activities of individuals or groups motivated by innate impulses. For the agitator these impulses are biological in nature, they function beyond and above history: Jews, for instance, are evil—a "fact" which the agitator simply takes for granted as an inherent condition that requires no explanation or development. Abstract intellectual theories do not seem to the masses as immediately "real" as their own emotional reactions. It is for this reason that the emotions expressed in agitation appear to function as an independent force, which exists prior to the articulation of any particular issue, is expressed by this articulation, and continues to exist after it. . . .

Malaise is a consequence of the depersonalization and permanent insecurity of modern life. Yet it has never been felt among people so strongly as in the past few decades. The inchoate protest, the sense of disenchantment and the vague complaints and forebodings that are already perceptible in late nineteenth century art and literature have been diffused into general consciousness. There they function as a kind of vulgarized romanticism, a *Weltschmerz in perpetuum,* a sickly sense of disturbance that is subterranean but explosive. The intermittent and unexpected acts of violence on the part of the individual and the similar acts of violence to which whole nations can be brought are indices of this underground torment. Vaguely sensing that something has gone astray in modern life but also strongly convinced that he lacks the power to right whatever is wrong, (even if it was possible to discover what is wrong), the individual lives in a sort of eternal adolescent uneasiness.

The agitator gravitates toward malaise like a fly to dung. He does not blink its existence as so many liberals do; he finds no comfort in the illusion that this is the best of all possible worlds. On the contrary, he grovels in it, he relishes it, he distorts and deepens and exaggerates the malaise to the point where it becomes almost a paranoiac relationship to the external world. For once the agitator's audience has been driven to this paranoic point, it is ripe for his ministrations. . . .

All such utilizations of malaise are possible only on condition that the audience does not become aware of its roots in modern society. The malaise remains in the background of agitation, the raw material of which is supplied by the audience's stereotyped projections of the malaise. Instead of trying to go back to their sources, to treat them as symptoms of a bad condition, the agitator treats them as needs that he promises to satisfy. He is therefore not burdened with the task of correcting the audience's inadequate ideas; on the contrary, he can let himself be carried along by its "natural" current.(7)

THE AGITATOR: THEMES AND PORTRAIT*

Which brings us to a portrait of the agitator, the comparison of his
techniques with those of other advocates of social change, and the essence
of his "line." The following excerpts are from *Prophets of Deceit*, including the sample agitator speech which, as noted in the original text, "is a
composite of actual statements made by American agitators. Except for
the punctuation, everything—words, thoughts, appeals—is all theirs."

Agitation may be viewed as a specific type of public activity
and the agitator as a specific type of "advocate of social
change." . . .

The immediate cause of the activity of an "advocate of social
change" is a social condition that a section of the population
ffeels to be iniquitous or frustrating. This discontent he articulates by pointing out its presumed causes. He proposes to defeat
the social groups held responsible for perpetuating the social
condition that gives rise to discontent. Finally, he promotes a
movement capable of achieving this objective, and he proposes
himself as its leader.

Here then are the four general categories under which the
output of any "advocate of social change" can be classified: Discontent, The Opponent, The Movement, and The Leader. Significant variations in the categories can be used to isolate sub-
classes; an especially useful division is to break down "advocate of social change" into "reformer" or "revolutionary," depending on whether the discontent is seen as circumscribed in
area or as involving the whole social structure.

Unlike the usual advocate of social change, the agitator, while
exploiting a state of discontent, does not try to define the nature
of that discontent by means of rational concepts. Rather does
he increase his audience's disorientation by destroying all rational guideposts and by proposing that they instead adopt
seemingly spontaneous modes of behavior. The opponent he
singles out has no discernibly rational features. His movement
is diffuse and vague, and he does not appeal to any well-defined
social group. He lays claim to leadership not because he understands the situation better than others but because he has suffered more than they have. The general purpose of his activity,
be it conscious or not, is to modify the spontaneous attitudes
of his listeners so that they become passively receptive to his
personal influence.

It is quite obvious that the agitator does not fit into the
reformer type; his grievances are not circumscribed, but on

---

* References at conclusion of this excerpt relate to internal footnotes.

the contrary take in every area of social life. Nor does he address himself to any distinct social group, as does the reformer; except for the small minority he brands as enemies, every American is his potential follower.

Yet he does not fit into the revolutionary group, either. While the discontent he articulates takes in all spheres of social life, he never suggests that in his view the causes of this discontent are inherent and inseparable from the basic social set-up. He refers vaguely to the inadequacies and iniquities of the existing social structure, but he does not hold it ultimately responsible for social ills, as does the revolutionary.

He always suggests that what is necessary is the elimination of people rather than a change in political structure. Whatever political changes may be involved in the process of getting rid of the enemy he sees as a means rather than an end. The enemy is represented as acting, so to speak, directly on his victims without the intermediary of a social form, such as capitalism is defined to be in socialist theory. For instance, although agitational literature contains frequent references to unemployment, one cannot find in it a discussion of the economic causes of unemployment. The agitator lays responsibility on an unvarying set of enemies, whose evil character or sheer malice is at the bottom of social maladjustment. . . .

Unlike the reformer or revolutionary the agitator makes no effort to trace social dissatisfaction to a clearly definable cause. The whole idea of objective cause tends to recede into the background, leaving only on one end the subjective feeling of dissatisfaction and on the other the personal enemy held responsible for it. As a result, his reference to an objective situation seems less the basis of a complaint than a vehicle for a complaint rooted in other, less visible causes.

This impression is confirmed when we observe with what facility the agitator picks up issues from current political discussions and uses them for his own purposes. Throughout the past sixteen years, despite the extraordinary changes witnessed in American life, the agitator kept grumbling and vituperating in the same basic tone. Unlike political parties, he never had to change his "general line." When unemployment was of general concern, he grumbled about that; when the government instituted public works to relieve unemployment, he joined those who inveighed against boondoggling. . . .

It should by now be clear that the agitator is neither a reformer nor a revolutionary. His complaints do refer to social reality but not in terms of rational concepts. When the reformer and revolutionary articulate the original complaint, they supplant predominating emotional by intellectual elements. The relationship between complaint and experience in agitation is rather indirect and nonexplicit.

The reformer and revolutionary generalize the audience's rudimentary attitudes into a heightened awareness of its predicament. The original complaints become sublimated and socialized. The direction and phychological effects of the agitator's activity are radically different. The energy spent by the reformer and revolutionary to lift the audience's ideas and emotions to a higher plane of awareness is used by the agitator to exaggerate and intensify the irrational elements in the original complaint.

The following incident illustrates the difference between the two approaches. In a crowded New York bus a woman complained loudly that she was choking, that she was pushed and squeezed by other passengers, and added that "something should be done about it." (*A typical inarticulate complaint.*) A second passenger observed: "Yes, it's terrible. The bus company should assign more busses to this route. If we did something about it, we might get results." (*The solution of a reformer or revolutionary. The inarticulate expression of the complainant is translated into an objective issue—in this case "the faulty organization of the transportation services that can be remedied by appropriate collective action."*) But then a third passenger angrily declared: "This has nothing to do with the bus company. It's all those foreigners who don't even speak good English. They should be sent back where they came from." (*The solution of the agitator who translates the original complaint not into an issue for action against an established authority, but into the theme of the vicious foreigners.*)

In contradistinction to all other programs of social change, the explicit content of agitational material is in the last analysis incidental—it is like the manifest content of dreams. The primary function of the agitator's words is to release reactions of gratification or frustration whose total effect is to make the audience subservient to his personal leadership.

It is true that the agitator sometimes appears to introduce concepts that were not originally present in the audience's complaints. But these are not the result of an objective analysis. When the agitator denounces government bureaucrats for the privations of wartime rationing, he does so not because he has discovered any causal relationship between the two but rather because he knows that there is a potential resentment against bureaucrats for reasons that have nothing to do with rationing. The appearance of an intellectual distance between the agitator and the audience is deceptive: instead of opposing the "natural" current, the agitator lets himself be carried by it. He neglects to distinguish between the insignificant and the significant; no complaint, no resentment is too small for the agitator's attention. What he generalizes is not an intellectual perception; what he produces is not the intellectual awareness of the predicament, but an aggravation of the emotion itself.

Instead of building an objective correlate of his audience's dissatisfaction, the agitator tends to present it through a fantastic and extraordinary image, which is an enlargement of the audience's own projections. The agitator's solutions may seem incongruous and morally shocking, but they are always facile, simple, and final, like daydreams. Instead of the specific effort the reformer and revolutionary demand, the agitator seems to require only the willingness to relinquish inhibitions. And instead of helping his follower to sublimate the original emotion, the agitator gives them permission to indulge in anticipatory fantasies in which they violently discharge those emotions against alleged enemies. . . .

The reformer or revolutionary concentrates on an analysis of the situation and tends to ignore irrational or subconscious elements. But the agitator appeals primarily to irrational or subconscious elements at the expense of the rational and analytical.(8)

The democratic leader usually tries to present himself as both similar to and different from his followers—similar in that he has common interests with them, different in that he has special talents for representing those interests. The agitator tries to maintain the same sort of relationship to his audiences, but instead of emphasizing the identity of his interests with those of his followers, he depicts himself as one of the plain folk, who thinks, lives and feels like them. In agitation this suggestion of proximity and intimacy takes the place of identification of interests.

The nature of the difference between leader and follower is similarly changed. Although the agitator intimates that he is intellectually and morally superior to his audience, he rests his claim to leadership primarily on the suggestion of his innate predestination. He does resort to such traditional American symbols of leadership as the indefatigable businessman and the rugged frontiersman, but these are overshadowed by the image he constructs of himself as a suffering martyr who, as a reward for his sacrifices, deserves special privileges and unlimited ascendancy over his followers. The agitator is not chosen by his followers but presents himself as their pre-chosen leader—pre-chosen by himself on the basis of a mysterious inner call, and pre-chosen as well by the enemy as a favorite target of persecution. One of the plain folk, he is yet far above them; reassuringly close, he is yet infinitely aloof.

While spokesmen for liberal and radical causes refrain, for a variety of reasons, from thrusting their own personalities into the foreground of their public appeals, the agitator does not hesitate to advertise himself. He does not depend on a "build-up" manufactured by subordinates and press agents, but does the job himself. He could hardly trust anyone else to paint his self-image in such glowing colors. As the good fellow who has nothing to hide, whose effusiveness and garrulousness know no limit, he does not seem to be inhibited by considerations of good taste from openly displaying his private life and his opinions about himself.

This directness of self-expression is particularly suitable for one who aspires to be the spokesman for those suffering from social malaise. The agitator seems to realize almost intuitively that objective argumentation and impersonal discourse would only intensify the feelings of despair, isolation, and distrust from which his listeners suffer and from which they long to escape. Such a gleeful display of his personality serves as an *ersatz* assertion of individuality. Part of the secret of his charisma as a leader is that he presents the image of a self-sufficient personality to his followers. If they are deprived of such a blessing, then at least they can enjoy it at second remove in their leader.

Those who suffer from malaise always want to pour their hearts out, but because of their inhibitions and lack of opportunities they seldom succeed. Conceiving of their troubles as individual and inner maladjustments, they want only a chance to be "understood," to clear up the "misunderstandings" which others have about them. On this need the agitator bases his own outpouring of personal troubles. When he talks about himself the agitator vicariously gratifies his followers' wish to tell the world of their troubles. He lends an aura of sanction and validity to the desire of his followers endlessly to complain, and thus his seemingly sincere loquacity strengthens his rapport with them. His trials are theirs; his successes also theirs. Through him they live.

By seemingly taking his listeners into his confidence and talking "man to man" to them, the agitator achieves still another purpose: he dispels any fear they may have that he is talking above their heads or against their institutionalized ways of life. He is the elder brother straightening things out for them, not a subversive who would destroy the basic patterns of their lives. The enemy of all established values, the spokesman of the apocalypse, and the carrier of disaffection creates the atmosphere of a family party in order to spread his doctrine the more effectively. Blending protestations of his weakness with intimations of his strength, he whines and boasts at the same time. Cannot one who is so frank about his humility also afford to be equally frank about his superiority?

The agitator's references to himself thus fall into two groups or themes: one covering his familiarity and the other his aloofness, one in a minor key establishing him as a "great little man," and the other in a major key as a bullet-proof martyr who despite his extraordinary sufferings always emerges victorious over his enemies.

GREAT LITTLE MAN: Unlike those idealists who, sacrificing comfort in behalf of a lofty social goal, "go to the people," the agitator somes from the people; in fact, he is always eager to show that socially he is almost indistinguishable from the great mass of American citizens. "I am an underdog who has suffered through the depression like most of the people."[1] Like millions of other Americans, he is "one of [those] plain old time, stump grubbing, liberty loving, apple cider men and women."[2] Yet he is always careful to make it clear that he is one of the endogamic *élite*, "an American-born citizen whose parents were American born and whose parents' parents were American born. I think that's far enough back."[3] There is no danger that anyone will discover he had an impure grandmother.

Not only is he one of the people, but his most ardent wish is always to remain one and enjoy the pleasures of private existence. He hates to be in the limelight, for he is "an old-fashioned American" who, he cheerfully admits, does not even know his "way around in the circles of high society at Washington."[4] If it were really up to him and if his conscience didn't tell him otherwise, he'd spend all his time on his favorite hobby: "If we had a *free* press in America I doubt if Gerald Smith would publish *The Cross and the Flag*. I am sure I wouldn't publish AMERICA PREFERRED. In my spare time I'd play golf."[5] Even when he finally does seek office, it is only after a heart-rending conflict and after he has received the permission of his parents: ". . . . first, I would have to get the consent of my Christian mother and father, because years ago I had promised them that I would not seek office."[6] And on those rare occasions when he can escape from his duties for a few minutes of relaxation, he proudly tells his listeners about it: "Well, friends, Lulu and

I managed to get time out to attend the annual carnival and bazaar of the Huntington Park Chapter of the Indoor Sports Club."[7]

Even at this rather uncomplicated level of identification the agitator is ambiguous. By his very protestations that he is quite the same as the mass of Americans he smuggles in hints of his exceptional status. Public life, he intimates, is a bother, and whoever deserts his private pleasures in its behalf must have some good reason for doing so. By constantly apologizing for his abandonment of private life and his absorption in public life, the agitator suggests that there are special provinces and unusual responsibilities that are limited to the uniquely endowed. If one of the plain people, such as he, gains access to such privileges and burdens, then it must surely be because of his unusual talents. He has embarked on a difficult task for which he is specially qualified, and therefore his followers owe him gratitude, admiration, and obedience.

A GENTLE SOUL. Although he is, by virtue of his special talents, a man who has risen out of the common people, the agitator remains a kindly, gentle soul—folksy, good-natured, golden-hearted. Far be it from him to hold any malice against any fellow human being, for "if we must hate, let us hate hate."[8] Nor is he "the kind of person who carries hatred or bitterness for any length of time . . . In spite of all I have gone through I have never lost my sense of humor, my ability to laugh, even right into the face of seeming disaster."[9]

Like all other Americans, he is a good and solicitous father to his children, and in a moment of difficulty appeals touchingly to his friends for help: "My son, 9½ years old, is pestering me, wanting a bicycle. Get in touch with me, please, if anyone knows where I could obtain a second-hand bicycle very cheap."[10] But his virtues come out most clearly in his role as model husband. He regales his audience with bits of intimate family dialogue: "I said one day to my sweet wife."[11] And even he, the would-be dictator, does not hesitate to admit that the little, or not so little, wife is the boss at home: "If I don't look out I'll be looking for a boss' lap on which to sit and chew gum. Well, Lulu's the boss and, having gained about 25 pounds during the past six months, she has plenty of lap on which to sit."[12]

As he makes the rounds of his meetings, his faithful wife accompanies him: "A few weeks ago found Mrs. Winrod and me spending Sunday at Sioux City, Iowa, holding meetings in the Billy Sunday Memorial Tabernacle."[13] And when he wishes to express his gratitude to his followers, it is again as the gentle soul, the faithful family man: "The wife and I are very grateful for the prayerful letters, kind words, and sums remitted so far . . ."[14] So sweet and lovable are both his personality and his family life that he offers family pictures for sale: "How many have received 1. Calendar of Mrs. Smith, me and Jerry? 2. A copy of my 'undelivered speech'?"[15]

TROUBLES SHARED. One of the agitator's favorite themes is his economic troubles, about which he speaks to complete strangers with perfect ease:

> I must confide to you without reservation . . . I have spent everything I have; I have surrendered every possession I had in this world in order to carry on this fight. I will not be able to borrow any more money; I have nothing left to sell.[16]

Another agitator complains that by engaging in political activity he has embarked on "a gamble with the security of my wife and children at stake."[17] And still another offers the audience a detailed financial statement:

> The taxes on my Kenilworth home are unpaid and there are some $1800 in outstanding bills accrued since I stopped depleting my few remaining securities, although I have paid light, phone and groceries . . . his [her husband's] refusal to give us any of the milk check income from my farm, his continuing to spend this income while associating with the woman he brought to sleep in my own bed at my farm, finally made it necessary to take some legal steps to protect the family.[18]

The agitator is just as frank about the condition of his health as about his financial or marital contretemps. We find him making great sacrifices that cause him to commiserate with himself: "I come home and say to Mrs. Smith, 'How does this old heart of mine keep up'? . . . But I know how men like that go—they go all of a sudden."[19] And even when his heart doesn't bother him, his teeth do: "The last time I saw Charlie Hudson, he still had been unable to afford to get needed dental work done. His wife takes roomers."[20] His afflictions threatened to handicap his political work.

> My dentist informed me I must have four teeth removed at once. I don't mind that so much as I do the fact that I may come on the air tomorrow, after the teeth have been extracted, and sound like a dear old gentleman who has been drawing old-age pension for forty years or more.[21]

By multiplying such references to his family, his health, and his finances, the agitator tries to create an atmosphere of homey intimacy. This device has immediate, gratifying implications. The personal touch, the similarity between agitator and audience, and the intimate revelations of "human interest" provide emotional compensation for those whose life is cold and dreary, especially for those who must live a routinized and atomized existence.

Equally gratifiying to listeners may be the fact that such revelations help satisfy their curiosity—a universal feature of contemporary mass culture. It may be due to the prevalent feeling that one has to have "inside information" that comes "from the horse's mouth" in order to get along in modern society. Perhaps, too, this curiosity is derived from an unconscious infantile desire to glimpse the forbidden life of the grown-ups—a desire closely related to that of revealing and enjoying scandals. When the listener is treated as an insider his libido is gratified, and it matters little to him whether he hears revelations about crimes and orgies supposedly indulged in by the enemy or about the increase in weight of the agitator's wife. He has been allowed to become one of those "in the know."

PUBLIC PRIVACY. When the agitator indulges in his uninhibited displays of domesticity and intimacy, he does so not as a private person but as a public figure. This fact endows his behavior with considerable ambivalence. His lyrical paeans in praise of the pleasure of private existence imply *ipso facto* a degrading of this privacy when he exposes it to public inspection. This gesture has the double meaning of an invasion of the agitator's private life by his public life and of his public life by his private life. In this way the traditional liberal differentiation between the two is made to seem obsolete and in any case untenable. Privacy is no longer possible in this harsh social world—except as a topic of public discussion.

Finally, these revelations of private life serve to enhance the agitator's stature as a public figure, who, it has already been suggested, vicariously symbolizes the repressed individualities of his adherents. He establishes his identity with the audience by telling it of his financial troubles and other kinds of failures, but he also underlines the fact of his success. He has risen from the depths in which the followers still find themselves; in contrast to them, he has managed to integrate his public and private personalities. The proof of this is simple enough—is he not talking to the followers and are they not listening to him? As a symbol of his followers' longings, the agitator centers all attention on himself, and soon his listeners may forget that he is discussing, not public issues, but his qualifications for leadership.

That the agitator simultaneously stresses his own weakness, that he pictures himself as all too human, does not impair the effectiveness of his attempt at self-exaltation. By the very fact that he admits his weaknesses while stressing his powers, he implies that the followers too can, if to a lesser extent, become strong once they surrender their private existence to the public movement.

They need but follow the path of the great little man.

BULLET-PROOF MARTYR: Aside from his remarkable readiness to share his troubles with his fellow men, what are the qualities that distinguish the great little man from the rest of the plain folk and make him fit to be one of "those . . . who lead"?[22] Here again the agitator is ready to answer the question. Although the agitator calls himself an old-fashioned Christian American, Christian humility is hardly one of his outstanding virtues. For all his insistence that he is one of the common folk, he does not hesitate to declare that he is an exceptionally gifted man who knows and even admires his own talent.

That he has no difficulty in overcoming conventional reticence about such matters is due not merely to his quite human readiness to talk about himself but also to the fact that his prominence is not merely his own doing. As he has emphasized, his natural inclination is not to lead humanity: he would rather play golf. But he cannot help it—forces stronger and more imperious than his own will push him to leadership. Both because of his innate dynamism and because he has been singled out by the enemy, the mantle of leadership, like it or not, falls on his shoulders.

THE INNER CALL. Suggesting that his activity is prompted by sacred command, the agitator speaks of himself as the "voice of the great unorganized and helpless masses."[23] He is "giving vocal expression to the thoughts that you have been talking about around your family tables."[24] But it also comes from holier regions: "Like John the Baptist," the agitator is "living just for the sweet privilege of being a voice in the wilderness."[25] As such, the agitator does not hesitate to compare himself to Christ: "Put down the Crown of Thorns on me."[26] He sees himself continuing the work of the "Divine Savior.[27]

But for all his suggestions that he has a divine responsibility the agitator does not pretend to bring any startlingly new revelation. He does not claim to make his audience aware of a reality that they see only partially; he does not claim to raise the level of their consciousness. All he does is to "say what you all want to say and haven't got the guts to say it."[28] What "others think . . . privately," the agitator says "publicly."[29] And for this purpose he is specially talented: as one agitator says of another, he delivered what was "perhaps the greatest address we have ever had on Christian statesmanship."[30]

Like a new Luther, he bellows defiance of established powers without regard to consequences: "I am going to say some things this afternoon that some people won't like, but I cannot help it, I must speak the truth."[31] Nothing can "halt and undo the inner-

most convictions of stalwart sons of Aryan blood,"[32] not even the
ingratitude of those who spurn him: "Nevertheless, there I will
stand demanding social justice for all even though some of the
ill-advised whom I am endeavoring to defend will take a pot-shot
at me from the rear."[33]

Nor is the agitator's courage purely spiritual:

> If the Gentiles of the nation back up Pelley now in his challenge to the
> usurpers of American liberties, they are going to get a "break" that they
> have never dreamed possible till Pelley showed the spunk to defy the
> nepotists.[34]

The agitator, aware of both his qualifications and his courage,
knows that

> When the history of America is written . . . concerning the preservation
> of the American way of life, I am going to be thankful that in the day
> when men were cowardly and overcautious and crawled under the bed and
> allowed themselves to be bulldozed by a bunch of wire-whiskered Com-
> munists and atheists and anti-God politicians, that there was one man by
> the name of Gerald L. K. Smith that had the courage to be an old-fash-
> ioned, honest to God, Christian American![35]

And the agitator knows too that his courage extends to somewhat smaller matters as well:

> When I went to the Auditorium, although it was very cold, probably
> five degrees below zero—twenty degrees the first time, five degrees the
> second time—the place was packed and every inch of standing room was
> taken. I had to pass through a picket line, one of those vicious picket lines
> organized by Reds and enemies of our meeting there.[36]

It is this blending of seriousness and unseriousness, of the sublime Crown of Thorns and the toothache that characterizes the
agitator's approach to composing his self-portrait as well as to the
other themes of his speeches and writings. He is both the little
man suffering the usual hardships and the prophet of truth:
Walter Witty and Jeremiah rolled up into one.

Such an indiscriminate mixture of trivial and sublime symbols
might appear blasphemous or simply disgusting, but the agitator
seems to count on a different kind of reaction. Instead of imposing
on his listeners the difficult task of following a saint, a task which
might after all cause them to feel that they too must assume some
of the traits of sainthood, he gratifies them by dragging the lofty
notions of sainthood down to a humdrum, *kleinbürgerlich* level.
The followers thereby are offered an object of admiration, the
image of the desanctified saint, that is closer to their own level
of feeling and perception. The agitator imposes no strain on them.

There is still another gratification for the audience in the agitator's narcissistic outbursts of self-praise. A courageous and self-
reliant man might be disgusted with the spectacle of someone

celebrating himself as the repository of all the manly virtues, but people who are acclimated to self-denial and self-hatred are paradoxically attracted by the selfish narcissist. As a leading psychoanalyst puts it: "This narcissistic behavior which gives the dependent persons no hope for any real love arouses their readiness for identification."* Accordingly, the agitator does not count on the support of people capable of self-criticism or self-reliance; he turns to those who constantly yearn for magical aids to buttress their personalities.

PERSECUTED INNOCENCE. Like any advocate of social change the agitator appeals to social frustration and suffering, but in his output there is a striking contrast between the vagueness with which he refers to the sufferings of his listeners as a social group and the vividness with which he documents his personal trials. He speaks as though the malaise resulted in tangible hardship in him alone. His trials and ordeals are truly extraordinary, almost superhuman, and by comparison the complaints of his followers seem merely to refer to minor nuisances, insignificant reflections of his glorious misfortunes. He is the chosen martyr of a great cause—himself. As they compare their lot to his, the followers cannot but feel that they are almost like safe spectators watching a battle between the forces of evil and their own champion of virtue.

In building up this image of persecuted innocence, the agitator uses religious symbols. He "has come through the most heartrending Gethsemane, I believe, of any living man in America today,"[37] and he does not hesitate to compare himself to the early Christian martyrs: "Many leaders . . . sneered at Father Coughlin and turned thumbs down on the Christian Fronters, as did the Patrician population of Rome turn their thumbs down on the Christian slave martyrs . . ."[38]

But these religious associations are only decorations for ordeals that are strictly secular; the agitator's sufferings are of this world. Here he runs into a difficulty. In actual fact, he has met with little interference from the public authorities.** Yet he realizes

I don't know what is going to happen to me. All I ask you to do is, don't be surprised at anything. If I am thrown in jail, if I am indicted, if I am smeared, if I am hurt physically, no matter what it might be, don't be surprised at anything, because everything in the calendar is now being attempted. . . . I am glad to make that sacrifice.[39]

---

* Fenichel, O.: The Psychoanalytical Theory of Neurosis, New York, Norton, 1945, p. 510.

** Except for those involved in the wartime sedition trial and one agitator convicted as an enemy agent, the American agitators have suffered only from exposures and criticism.

that as a man with a mission, he must be persecuted. If the past will yield no evidence, perhaps the future will, for who is to deny him the right to premonitions:

One reason why the agitator has difficulty in specifying the persecutions to which he is subjected is that his enemies work in secret. They force him to the most surreptitious behavior: "I, an American, must sneak in darkness to the printer to have him print my booklet and to get it out to the people like a bootlegger."[40] He is beset by vague dangers that are difficult to pin down: "One of these newspapermen, according to another newspaperman, is said to have predicted somewhat as follows: 'Two Jews from England were over here to see that Hudson does not get home alive.' "[41]

But when the agitator gets down to bedrock, it becomes clear that what he most resents is public criticism, which he describes as "smearing" and "intimidation." He complains that "Jewish New-Dealers in the Congress . . . started a mighty ball rolling to smear Pelley from the scene."[42] And "because I dare to raise my voice foreigners are intimidating me and trying to ge me off the air."[43] Nor does he feel happy that "frequently we have heard it prophesied over the radio by such noble patriots as Walter Winchell and others, that we were about to be incarcerated in concentration camps."[44]

A SLIGHT CASE OF MURDER. However insubstantial the evidence he can summon for his martyrdom, the agitator, it must be admitted, works it for all it is worth. He continually suggests that he has embarked on a dangerous career and that he is actually risking his life. The threat never abates, as we shall see in tracing it during the course of one agitator's statements over a period of twelve years.

As early as October, 1936, he realized that his death warrant had been signed. Like his political boss, who was assassinated, ". . . it may cost my life."[45] And not without reason: "Ten threats came to me within twenty-four hours here in New York City."[46]

Three years later these threats of murder were still harassing him: "I continued to receive all sorts of threats against my life . . ."[47]

By 1942 the rather slow-working murderers had a definite objective: to keep him out of the Senate. "I am convinced that there are men in America who would rather commit murder than see me in the United States Senate."[48] Other murderers, or perhaps the same ones, found his literary output more objectionable than the possibility of his becoming a Senator: "I have been warned that I will not live to complete this series of articles."[49]

Half a year passes, and the enemy is still intent on murder. "A certain set of ruthless men in this nation have actually called for my assassination."[50] The murderers seem finally to have worked up enough energy or courage to come within striking distance:

I held a meeting down in Akron, Ohio, one time and my Committee resigned the afternoon of the meeting . . . I had to walk into that armory alone . . . I walked from the hotel over to this place which seated about 6,000 people alone, and when I got over there, the place was packed . . . I walked down the center aisle, walked right up to the microphone and the first thing I said was this, "There are men in this room who would like to see me killed tonight" . . .[51]

Yet even then there is no record of the murderers doing anything. Two more years went by and by the spring of 1945 the still healthy agitator noted that the threat to his life had become so real that it was even confirmed by police authorities: "Shortly before the end of the meeting I received a message from the police detectives to the effect that they were convinced that there was a definite plot to de me great injury, perhaps kill me."[52] Nothing seems to have come of that danger, but by the summer of the same year the agitator reported that "people who know what is going on are convinced that a plan is on foot to actually get me killed at the earliest possible moment."[53] As of the moment of writing, the agitator remains alive and unharmed, never having once been the victim of assault or assassination. As late as April 29, 1948, he still maintained that he was the object of an attempt on his life, this time by means of "arsenic poisoning."[54]

That he has no genuine factual data to support his charges does not seem to disturb the agitator: he persists in believing that an evil force is out to get him. His recital of fears, smearing, premonitions, anonymous letters—all this adds up to the familiar picture of paranoia. The paranoiac's conviction that he is persecuted cannot be logically refuted since it is itself extralogical. In agitation the leader acts out, as it were, a complete case history of persecution mania before his listeners, whose own inclinations to regard themselves as the target of persecution by mysterious forces is thus sanctioned and encouraged. Nevertheless it is the agitator who remains at the center of the stage; it is on him that all the imaginary enemy blows fall. By symbolically taking upon himself all the burdens of social suffering, he creates unconscious guilt feelings among his followers, which he can later exploit by demanding their absolute devotion as recompense for his self-sacrifice. And since the enemy exacts the heaviest penalty from him, he has the implicit right to claim the highest benefits once the enemy is defeated. Similarly, since the enemy singles him out for persecution, he has the right to engage in terroristic reprisals. All of these consequences follow from the agitator's self-portrait-as martyr.

But simultaneously the agitator, for all the dangers to which he is exposed, does manage to survive and continue his work. He is not merely the martyr but also the remarkably efficient leader, and on both counts he deserves special obedience. Since he is both more exposed and better equipped than his followers, his claims to leadership are doubly vindicated.

THE MONEY-MINDED MARTYR. There are many indications that, at its present stage at least, American agitation is a racket as well as a political movement. To what extent the agitator actually depends on his followers' financial contributions it is difficult to say with any degree of certainty. In any event he does not account for the use of the money he collects. It seems probable that at least some agitators have been heavily subsidized by anonymous wealthy donors, while it is known that some of the smaller fry make a living by selling their literature.

When the agitator appeals to his followers for money, he strengthens their devotion to the cause by leading them to make financial sacrifices. In agitation such psychological factors are probably of greater importance than in other movements. For it must be remembered that in agitation the follower has no precise idea what his cause is, that the whole background of the agitator's appeal is one of destruction and violence, with a meager minimum of positive stimuli. What remains then is the agitator himself—his inflated personality and his pressing needs. The agitator does not hesitate to act the insistent beggar. He begs meekly: "Oh, I'm just a common American citizen, friends, poor in the world's gifts, depending on the quarters and dollars of friends and radio listeners."[55] But he also begs for himself as the agent of history: "It is a long grind to get the thousands of dollars absolutely necessary as a minimum in this way. But it must be done if the fight is to go on."[56] "Why hold back your financial aid NOW—when revolution itself is being shouted from our public rostrums?"[57]

He begs for aid, but he also warns that those who do not come through now may live to regret it: "If any of you don't agree with the principles of America First and don't care to contribute to our cause, this is the time for you to get up and walk out."[58] Those who do not comply face the dreaded penalty of exclusion —they have to walk out and be alone with themselves.

MAGIC OF SURVIVAL. That he has managed to survive under terrible financial handicaps and political persecution arouses the agitator's self-admiration. ". . . How could he emerge unscathed with such colossal forces arrayed to smash him?"[59] His invulnerability is remarkable and is only slightly short of miraculous. His safety is, in fact, adduced as proof that he has gone through dangers, and as he concludes his report of the plot hatched against him by English Jews, he remarks with a note of defiance in his voice: "I arrived safely Sunday night."[60] His life seems to him protected by an anonymous providence: ". . . *Pelley is an absolute fatalist . . . he believes that nothing can harm him until he has done the work which he came into life at this particular period to do!*"[61] And he always returns to the fight: "I intend to . . . toss off the shackles that have been thrown around me . . . to spread my wings again . . .and to soar to new heights to carry on the battle."[62] For his powers of exertion are tremendous: "I speak two hours here and two hours there, and write all night and talk all day to people and write letters and work and . . . and everything else, and still I always seem to have the strength to do what lies before me."[63]

Seen from one persepctive, all this bragging is rather harmless A narcissist naturally believes himself invulnerable and omnipotent, and his slightly posturings only endear him to his audience. He is reduced to a level that is within their vision. Like the extraordinary exploits of the hero of a movie or a cheap novel, the agitator's adventure ends up an ultimately happy note —the hero is saved. From this harmless relapse into an adolescent atmosphere, the followers, together with the agitator himself, draw a certain simple gratification. They have been in the company of a hero who is not too heroic to be akin to them.

And yet somewhere in this interstices of this harmless braggadocio there lurk the grimmer notes of violence and destruction. The agitator's self-portrait of miraculous survival has a solid reality basis; he really does enjoy a high degree of impunity. He is safe and sound, magically immune, secretly protected—and this despite his verbal violence and scurrilous denunciations of the powers that be or of some of the powers that be. If his enemies do not carry out their threats of murder, it is not because they would not want to but because they do not dare. Their power, the agitator thereby suggests, is rather less impressive than it appears; they have only the façade of power. Real power is on his side.

Behind this definance of the enemy's threats lurks another suggestion: when the hour strikes and the seemingly strong enemy is revealed in his true weakness, the agitator will take revenge for the torments of fear that have been imposed on him. Perhaps it is not too bold to conjecture that as the agitator continually stresses his own bodily vigor, he is implicitly developing a complementary image to his leading metaphor of the enemy as a Low Animal. His own body is indestructible, but the helpless bodies of the enemy—those parasitical and disease-breeding low animals—are doomed to destruction. Behind the whining complaints and the triumphant self-admiration of this indestructible martyr looms the vision of the eugenic storm troops. The agitator is a good little guy, to be sure; he is a martyr who suffers endlessly; he survives by virtue of superior destines; but in the long run he makes sure to protect himself.

TOUGH GUY. The agitator knows that sometimes he must bare his teeth. Often he does it with the air of a youthful gang leader testing his hoodlums:

I am going to test my people. I am going to see if the fathers that left their bones on the desert had real sons. I am going to find out if the children of the men that rebuilt San Francisco after the earthquake are real men.[64]

Such vague anticipations of the agitator's future role are supplemented with more direct hints about his present strength. He means business, even if he is a great little man. "I am a tough guy. I am tough because I have got the goods on them."[65] The easy-going braggart is also a brutal swashbuckler. "They can threaten me all they want to. I am not a damned bit afraid to walk the streets of New York all by myself. I don't have to. I have the toughest men in New York with me."[66] Nor does he always have to sneak in the dark to his printer: "Huskies of my 'American Group' protect me when I take my printed booklets from the printer's plant."[67]

The bodyguard, however, is used not merely against the enemy. The same bodyguard that protects the leader from the enemy also protects him from any interference from his listeners: Their role is to listen, not to participate. When he speaks, you had better listen—or else. In this way the agitator already establishes himself as a constituted authority. The agitator brags about this:

So as we moved down through the middle of the meeting I said, "Now, we are not going to have any disturbance, we are not going to be heckled and the first man who attempts that, we will throw him out through the nearest window." So one fellow like this boy, way up in the balcony said something and somebody didn't understand what he said and he was almost pitched out of the window.[68]

It is in this atmosphere, in which even the followers are threatened with manhandling if they step out of line, that the agitator tests out a future device: the totalitarian plebiscite. "Do you authorize me to send a telegram to Senator Reynolds . . . put up your hands . . . All right, that is number one."[69] He feeds them cues: "I bid for the American vote under that flag. Give that a hand."[70] Such presentiments of the plebiscite are in themselves trivial enough, but they serve to emphasize the agitator's role as the sole legitimate voice to which everyone must listen in silence except when told to speak up in unison.

INSIDE KNOWLEDGE. Not only is the agitator physically powerful and something of a terrorist to boot, but he also has access to secret and highly important information, the source of which he is most careful not to reveal. He quotes mysterious "sources" that enabled him to "correctly diagnose 3 years ago that the 1940 presidential election would not be bonafide . . ."[71] He claims that "there has fallen into my hands a copy of these confidential instructions which came out from New York City concerning the underground science."[72] By miraculous but unspecified means he manages to penetrate into the heart of the enemy fortress where his sharp ears hear the confidences that "Zionists in America whispered within secret circles . . ."[73]

On other occasions the agitator can offer only promises of revelations to come: "I sall try to keep you posted concerning the diabolical conspiracy."[74] Or his information is too horrible to disclose: "I personally have had some experiences in the last year that would make your blood run cold, if I could tell you what they were."[75] Or he is bound by professional secrecy:

Two contacts, best unnamed on account of nature of information divulged, inform: ". . . believes that he has discovered the hdqtrs. of what seems to be Grand Orient Masonry . . . uptown in New York City. A building in the middle of a large block, surrounded by apartment houses; in a sort of courtyard, with a high barbed wire fence around it. No one is ever seen to enter this place, altho access could be had underground from one or more of the surrounding houses. A large telephone cable, sufficient for over 100 lines, goes to the place which is guarded night and day by armed guards . . ."[76]

The agitator uses the language of an adoslescent gang leader. He seeks to ingratiate himself with his listeners by promising them some highly important information. Some day the listeners will be "let in." But the agitator uses this technique of innuendo in ways other than the relatively harmless promise to divulge secrets. He withholds information in the very gesture by which he seems to give it out. He reveals not secrets but the existence of secrets; the secrets themselves are another variety of "forbidden fruit." Those affected by the promise to be "let in" are even more affected by the fact that the agitator has access to information inaccessible to them. To listen to innuendo and to rely on deliberately vague statements requires a certain readiness to believe, which the agitator directs towards his own person. So long as he does not reveal the "sources" of his knowledge, the agitator can continue to command the dependence of his followers. Unlike the educator, he never makes himself superfluous by revealing his methods of gaining knowledge. He remains the magical master.

This secret knowledge, like his toughness, is a two-edged weapon. It implies an ever present threat from which no one is quite safe: "Some day that thing is really going to come out, and when it comes out it is going to smell so high that any man that is connected with them, with that outfit, will be ashamed to say that he ever knew them."[77] or: "I have written a letter containing some mighty important information which I have placed in the hands of attorneys in this city. . . . The letter will not be printed . . . if we arrive home safely at the end of our campaign."[78]

Behind such statements there is the suggestion that he knows more than he says, and that nothing can ultimately remain hidden from him. If his self-portrait as a tough guy anticipates the storm trooper, then his insistence on his "inside knowledge" anticipates the secret files of the totalitarian police, which are used less against the political enemy, known in any case, than as a means to keep the followers in line. Sternly the agitator indicates this to his followers: get used to the idea now, if you want a share in this racket, you have to obey its rules—and I make the rules.

THE CHARISMATIC LEADER. The self-portrait of the agitator may seem a little ridiculous. Such an absurd creature—at once one of the plain folk and the sanctified leader; the head of a bedraggled family and a man above all material considerations; a helpless victim of persecution and a dreaded avenger with fists of iron! Yet contemporary history teaches us that this apparently ridiculous braggart cannot be merely laughed away.

In establishing this ambivalent image of himself the agitator achieves an extremely effective psychological result. In him, the martyr ultimately triumphant over his detractors and persecutors, the adherents see all their own frustrations magically metamorphosed into grandiose gratifications. They who are marginal suddenly have a prospect of sharing in the exceptional; their suffering now can appear to them as a glorious trial, their anonymity and servitude as stations on the road to fame and mastery. The agitator finds the promise of all these glories in that humdrum existence of his followers which had driven them to listen sympathetically to his appeals; he shows them how all the accumulated stuff of repression and frustration can be lit up into a magnificent fireworks, how the refuse of daily drudgery can be converted into a high explosive of pervasive destruction.

The self-portrait of the agitator is thus a culmination of all his other themes, which prepare the audience for the spectacle of the great little man acting as leader. Taking advantage of all the weaknesses of the present social order, the agitator intensifies his listeners' sense of bewilderment and helplessness, terrifies them with the specter of innumerable dangerous enemies and reduces their already crumbling individualities to bundles of reactive responses. He drives them into a moral void in which their inner voice of conscience is replaced by an externalized conscience: the agitator himself. He becomes the indispensable guide in a confused world, the center around which the faithful can gather and find safety. He comforts the sufferers of malaise, takes over the responsibility of history and becomes the exterior replacement of their disintegrated individuality. They live through him. (9)

THE AGITATOR SPEAKS

When will the plain, ordinary, sincere, sheeplike people of America awaken to the fact that their common affairs are being arranged and run for them by aliens, Communists, crackpots, refugees, renegades, Socialists, termites, and traitors? These alien enemies of America are like the parasitic insect which lays his egg inside the cocoon of a butterfly, devours the larvae and, when the cocoon opens, instead of a butterfly we find a pest, a parasite.

Oh, this is a clever scheme and if the American people don't get busy and fight it the whole vicious thing will be slipped over on you without your knowing what hit you. A comprehensive and carefully planned conspiracy, directed by a powerfully organized clique, and operating through official and semiofficial channels, has been in continuous existence since the days of Nimrod of Babylon, and is the ever lurking enemy of the people's liberty. Remember at all times that the tactics employed by these usurpers of Christian liberties will be to create horror and panic by exhibitions of maximum brutalities. (How would you like to have the bloodstream of your baby, or your son, or daughter, or wife polluted by dried blood collected from Jews, Negroes, and criminals?) It will be only ordinary sense at the first announcements of trouble for all householders to have several receptacles for storing drinking water on their premises so that ravages of thirst may not add to the general ordeal.

Hitler and Hitlerism are the creatures of Jewry and Judaism. The merciless programs of abuse which certain Jews and their satellites work upon people who are not in full agreement with them create terrible reactions. I am not justifying the reactions and I am not condoning the reactions; I am merely explaining them. Have the Jews forgotten that the more they organize materially against their opponents, the more assaults will increase and the closer they are to persecution?

Remember, these Jews expect to show no mercy to Christians. What is to prevent Jewish gangsters from doing damage to synagogues on purpose so as to create apparent justification for retaliation—in which Christian Americans, who know too much and have displayed too much courage, would be picked up dead in or near synagogues?

We know what the stuffed shirts and reactionaries will say. They will say we are crackpots. They will say that this program will appeal only to the lunatic fringe. But surely it is not anti-Semitism to seek the truth. Or is it?

What's wrong? I'll tell you what is wrong. We have robbed man of his liberty. We have imprisoned him behind the iron bars of bureaucratic persecution. We have taunted the American businessman until he is afraid to sign his name to a pay check for fear he is violating some bureaucratic rule that will call for the surrender of a bond, the appearance before a committee, the persecution before some Washington board, or even imprisonment itself.

While we have dissipated and persecuted management, we have stood idly by and watched a gang of racketeers, radicals, and conspirators regiment our workers in the name of organized labor into a dues-paying consipracy designed in Moscow to recruit workers for what they hope would become the American Red Revolution.

We are going to take this government out of the hands of these city-slickers and give it back to the people that still believe that 2 and 2 is 4, that God is in his heaven and the Bible is the Word. Down must come those who live in luxury, the laws that have protected the favored few, and those politicians who are disloyal to the voters!

Whenever a legislative body meets, liberties of the people are endangered by subtle and active interests. Lust for power, financial and political, is the ever-lurking enemy of the people's liberty. There is a deserved odium resting upon the word "liberal." Whether applied to Religion, Morals, or

Politics, "Liberalism" is destructive of all fundamental values. In matters pertaining to Religion, Liberalism leads to Atheism. In Morals, it leads to Nudism. In Politics, it leads to Anarchy. In the framework of a democracy the great mass of decent people do not realize what is going on when their interests are betrayed. This is a day to return to the high road, to the main road that leads to the preservation of our democracy and to the traditions of our republic.

Alien-minded plutocrats roll in wealth, bathe in liquor, surround themselves with the seduced daughters of America, and cooperate in all schemes to build up pro-Communist and anti-Christian sentiments. America, the vain—America, the proud—America, the nation of gluttons and spenders and drinkers. When Harry Hopkins got married, Mr. Baruch arranged the party. There were seven kinds of meat served—twenty-two kinds of food, and it had cost Barney Baruch $122 a plate; and they drank of the vintage of '26. You talk about the drunken orgies of history—we expect Capone to live like that, but as long as I am a Christian soul, I will not be governed by a man like that. That's what they do not want me to say. That's why I am such a bad man. Because I say what you all want to say and haven't got the guts to say.

We leaders are risking our lives to write a new page in American history. We propose without further ado, without equivocation, without any silly sentimentality sometimes known as Tolerance, to emasculate the debauchers within the social body and reestablish America on a basis where this spoliation can never again be repeated. I am attempting to speak one hundred times between the sixth of August and the fifteenth of September. This would be physically impossible for most men but thanks to the temperate and Christian life of my mother and father, I have been given a strong body and strong constitution. Even so, there will be nights that I will drop to the bed almost like a dead man, I will be so fatigued and exhausted. But I'll never throw mud at my opponent . . . I am led by the ethics and morals of Christ.

We are coming to the crossroads where we must decide whether we are going to preserve law and order and decency or whether we are going to be sold down the river to these Red traitors who are undermining America.

This meeting is not a lecture course, it is not an open forum . . . we are making history here today. This is a crusade. I don't know how we can carry on without money. All we want is money from enthusiastic friends.(10)

REFERENCES

(1) Phelps, Los Angeles, Sept. 26, 1940, radio.

(2) Smith, New York, Oct. 20, 1936, meeting.

(3) Phelps, Los Angeles, Aug. 7, 1941.

(4) Smith, *The Hoop of Steel*, p. 23.

(5) AP, May, 1945, p. 8.

(6) CF, May 1942, p. 8.

(7) Phelps, Los Angeles, July 28, 1941, radio.

(8) Coughlin, Speech on Jan. 29, 1939, reprinted in *Why Leave Our Own*, p. 57.

(9) Phelps, Los Angeles, July 21, 1941, radio

(10) Phelps, Los Angeles, Sept. 19, 1940, radio.

(11) Smith, New York, Oct. 20, 1936, meeting.

(12) Phelps, Los Angeles, Aug. 1, 1941.

(13) Winrod, *Letter*, Feb., 1943, p. 3.

(14) Hudson, letter to subscribers of his Bulletin, July, 1942.

(15) Smith, Detroit, Apr. 9, 1942, meeting.

(16) Smith, *Why is America Afraid?*

(17) Phelps, Los Angeles, Aug. 18, 1940, radio.

(18) RTL, Feb., 28, 1942, p. 3.

(19) Smith, Detroit, Mar. 19, 1943, meeting.

(20) PRB, Apr. 8, 1942, p. 1.

(21) Phelps, Los Angeles, Jan. 14, 1941, radio.

(22) CF, July,1945, p. 604.

(23) CF, May, 1942, p. 9.

(24) Stewart, New York, July 13, 1940, street corner.

(25) Smith, Cleveland, May 11, 1943, meeting.

(26) Smith, Detroit, Apr. 9, 1942, meeting.

(27) DEF, Oct., 1942, p. 11.

(28) Smith, St. Louis, Mar. 25, 1944, meeting.

(29) SJ, July 7, 1941,p. 4.

(30) CF, Aug., 1945, p. 616.

(31) Smith, *Why Is America Afraid?*

(32) LIB, Sept. 21, 1939, p. 7.

(33) SJ, June 5, 1939, p. 2.

(34) RC, Oct. 20, 1941, p. 16.

(35) Smith, Detroit, Mar. 19, 1943, meeting.

(36) Smith, *ibid.*

(37) DEF, Nov., 1940, p. 5.

(38) SJ, July 7, 1941, p. 4.

(39) Smith, Detroit, Mar. 19, 1943, meeting.

(40) Phelps, Los Angeles, No. 20, 1940, radio.

(41) AID, June 23, 1942, p. 4.

(42) Pelley, *What you Should Know About The Pelley Publications*, p. 4.

(43) Phelps, Los Angeles, Sep. 29, 1940, radio.

(44) Smith, Detroit, Mar. 22, 1943, meeting.

(45) Smith, New York, Oct. 20, 1936, meeting.

(46) Smith, *ibid.*

(47) Smith, *"Reds On The Run,"* radio, p. 2.

(48) CF, May, 1942, p. 9.

(49) CF, Oct.-Nov., 1942, p. 3.

(50) CF, Feb., 1943, p. 154.

(51) Smith, Detroit, Feb. 7, 1943, meeting.

(52) CF, Apr., 1945, p. 557.

(53) Smith, *Letter*, "The Battle of Babylon," July, 1945, p. 1.

(54) Smith, St. Louis, April 29, 1948, meeting.

(55) Phelps, Los Angeles, Sept. 8, 1940, radio.

(56) PRB, Aug. 10, 1942, p. 5.

(57) SJ, Nov. 27, 1939, p. 19.

(58) Smith, St. Louis, Mar. 25, 1944, meeting.

(59) *Pelley, What You Should Know About The Pelley Publications,* p. 5.

(60) AID, June 23, 1942, p. 4.

(61) Pelley, *Official Despatch*, p. 4.

(62) Phelps, Los Angeles, Dec. 31, 1940, radio.

(63) Smith, Detroit, Mar. 19, 1943, meeting.

(64) Smith, New York, Oct. 20,

1936, meeting.

(65) Phelps, Los Angeles, Oct. 8, 1940, radio.

(66) McWilliams, New York, July 29, 1940, street corner.

(67) Phelps, Los Angeles, Nov. 12, 1940, radio.

(68) Smith, Detroit, Feb. 7, 1943, meeting.

(69) Smith, Detroit, Mar. 19, 1943, meeting.

(70) Smith, New York, Oct. 20, 1936, meeting.

(71) AID, Jan. 19, 1942, p. 4.

(72) Smith, *"Dictatorship Comes with War,"* radio, p. 3.

(73) SJ, July 14, 1941, p. 7.

(74) Smith, *Letter,* Mar., 1943.

(75) CF, Feb., 1943, p. 154.

(76) AID, Nov. 26, 1941, p. 2.

(77) Smith, New York, Oct. 20, 1936, meeting.

(78) Phelps, Los Angeles, Feb. 7, 1941, radio.

SECTION II

STUDIES IN HATE

STUDIES IN HATE

THE SWASTIKA DAUBINGS

On December 24, 1959, a swastika was painted on a synagogue in Cologne, Germany. On December 26, the first of a wave of similiar incidents occurred in the United States. For some nine weeks thereafter, swastikas were smeared on Jewish temples, Jewish community centers, Jewish homes, on churches, on sidewalks, on college campuses, on automobiles Anti-Semitic slogans, sometimes in German, appeared on the walls of schoolrooms and on store-fronts. Bricks were hurled through the windows of synagogues, anonymous phone calls threatened bombings—and some of these threats were carried out. By the time the epidemic had passed, some 643 incidents had occurred.

Two organizations deeply concerned with manifestations of anti-Semitism and neo-Nazi behavior, the American Jewish Committee and the Anti-Defamation League, both undertook extensive investigation into the incidents, culminating in extensive psychological exploration into the backgrounds, emotional behavior and motivations of some of the youths apprehended. Both organizations published their findings in pamphlet form —the ADL in *Swastika, 1960* by David Caplovitz and Candace Rogers; the AJC in *Why the Swastika?*, a pamphlet prepared by staff member, Ann G. Wolfe. Both studies point up the manner in which the mechanism of prejudice was triggered, making of this series of incidents a "study in hate." The material which follows is virtually the total text of the American Jewish Committee pamphlet, paired with the concluding analysis of the Anti-Defamation League study.

Analysis of the incidents

The findings reported here are based on an analysis of 91 incidents in New York City, starting December 29, 1959, and continuing into March 1960. Of the 102 cases of vandalism and related offenses recorded by the police during the period, only those were studied which fell unmistakably into one of the following categories:

—Malicious defacement or destruction of religious property.

—Bomb threats against religious institutions.

—Daubing or marking of swastikas or anti-Semitic slogans on any property.

—Assault or threatened assault on Jewish individuals or groups.

—Defamatory or threatening letters sent to Jewish individuals or groups.

The chief facts about the episodes examined are as follows:
—As elsewhere in the nation, the largest number of incidents occurred during January.
—Contrary to initial expectations, the majority of cases were reported in neighborhoods with low, rather than high, delinquency rates.
—Vandalism was by far the most frequent offense, constituting more than 75 per cent of the episodes. Bomb scares accounted for less than 14 per cent; assault or threats of assault for less than 5 per cent.
—About 74 per cent of the offenses were directed against Jewish targets.
—Sixty-nine per cent of the incidents occurred in neightborhoods with a high proportion of Jewish residents.

Although many of the acts were superficially similar, closer scrutiny showed that they varied greatly in motivation. This was particularly true of the numerous cases of vandalism.

Offenses of this kind are of two distinct types. One is *wanton vandalism*—mischief-making of the kind that occurs as part of children's play. A typical case among those studied was the stoning of windows in a religious edifice by a groups of boys simply to see "who was the best shot."

Sharply distinct from the wanton variety is *vindictive vandalism*—a deliberate expression of hostility toward minority groups. Swastikas or anti-Jewish slogans painted on walls come under this heading.

About 60 per cent of the episodes, involving more than half of the offenders, were blatantly anti-Semitic and vindictive. The remaining 40 per cent appeared to have been pranks and were classified as wanton; many might not have come to the attention of the police if the atmosphere had not been charged with concern about vandalism against religious targets.

The majority of offenses committed by youths aged 16 to 21, including bomb scares and actual or threatened assault, were plainly anti-Semitic; in the acts committed by younger boys anti-Semitism was considerably less evident.

Only one of the offenses in New York City was the work of a single boy; all the others were committed by small or large groups. It is therefore necessary to understand the varieties of friendships and associations usually found among children and teen-agers.

Up to about 12 years of age, chidren spontaneously organize themselves into informal *play groups*. Membership constantly changes as boys and girls meet on the street, in school yards and playgrounds. Except for occasional minor squabbles, conflict with other groups is not featured.

Next come teen-age *neighborhood cliques,* more tightly knit and intimate, and usually restricted to boys of roughly equal status, who cling to one another with fierce loyalty. Fighting with other groups is not their main interest, even though cliques of different ethnic backgrounds are often embroiled in neighborhood conflicts.

Still more cohesive are the *gangs* formed by teen-age boys. While sometimes growing out of play groups or neighborhood cliques, gangs differ from them in having distinct traditions and goals. Gangs are less restrictive than neighborhood cliques in that they usually admit boys of varied status, but their organization tends to be tighter and more formal, with leaders who control admission and assign roles. These closely knit groups frequently offer an outlet to the youngster who cannot act out his hostilities alone. In the gang, hostility may be directed against parents, police or persons of status in the community; sometimes it is expressed in open warfare with other gangs.

When the offenders in New York, plus those belonging to the neo-Nazi group in the second city studied, are sorted out by group allegiances, the following picture emerges:

—Of the youths guilty of *vindictive,* anti-Semitic vandalism, two-thirds belonged to gangs or near-gangs, one-third to neighborhood cliques. Play groups were not involved in these acts.

—*Wanton* vandalism, on the other hand, was never the work of gangs. Play groups were responsible for one-third of the cases, neighborhood cliques for the rest.

The analysis shows, then, the vindictive acts against minority groups usually are the work of the more closely knit types of youth groups—those likely to give direction to the hostile impulses of their members.

The offenders' backgrounds

"I can't believe it . . . I can't believe it," a father exclaimed upon learning that his 16-year-old son had painted a swastika on the driveway of a Jewish family in Long Island, New York. A neighbor said, "He's a model boy. . . ."

"He loved art and hated violence . . . he couldn't have done a thing like that," insisted the parents of another 16-year-old, who was arrested for painting swastikas on a synagogue in Atlanta a few months before the wave of such acts broke out.

"Most of the twelve youths who tormented a Jewish couple over a period of 15 months are from . . . 'better families,' " a

San Francisco newspaper report states. "Some were in college or plan to enroll. . . . Some go to church regularly. . . . They looked and acted like Explorer Scouts, clean-cut, alert, 'normal.'"

These are the "nice" boys from the "better families," who engaged in swastika daubings, desecrations of houses of worship, and molestation of Jewish neighbors. On the surface, they look like "typical" American youngsters. Seeing one of them on the street, one would scarcely suspect that he could engage in violence or in the ugly anti-Semitic episodes which shocked the nation.

What are these boys really like? How did they come to engage in this species of activity? To explore these questions, the research team analyzed a wide range of facts bearing on the backgrounds, natural endowments and previous histories of those apprehended in New York City.

Except for one Negro and one Puetro Rican, all were white. About 50 per cent of the whites were of Irish descent, 22 per cent of Italian and 7 per cent of German descent.

Only one boy had an I.Q. below the average range, and several rated well above. Thus, whatever might lie at the root of their behavior, it was not low intelligence.

Because the swastika incidents were widely thought to be part of a general upswing of juvenile delinquency, the boys' histories were checked for earlier offenses. Data was gathered from records of previous court appearances—the index most commonly used by the FBI and social agencies, though by no means the only proof of prior delinquency.

It was found that 13 per cent of the offenders had been in court before, either once or repeatedly; 75 per cent had not. (No information could be obtained for the remaining 12 per cent.) Previous delinquency seems to have been limited almost entirely to the older boys (between 16 and 21), about half of whom had court records.

The children (9 to 15) also differed from the youths (16 to 21) in socio-economic background. The wage earners in the children's families were skilled or semi-skilled workers or laborers, except for one teacher. In contrast, the fathers of the older boys included a physician, the owner of a small business and several skilled technicians.

For the most part, the older boys lived in moderate-income, rather than economically depressed, neighborhoods; 86 per cent had their homes in areas where the median yearly family income was $3,800. Here again, the children were less favored than the youths.

The home neighborhoods were not conspicuous for juvenile

delinquency; only 9 per cent of all the offenders came from areas with delinquency rates that could be considered high.

As for the religious composition of neighborhoods, 73 per cent of the boys lived in sections with a high proportion of Jews. A similar picture, incidentally, was found in the nation as a whole; the frequency of incidents was more consistently related to the size of the Jewish population in the area than to any other factor, being high in states with many Jewish residents, and low in states with few.

Altogether, then, the environment in most cases might be described as roughly average or standard—free from destitution and from delinquency-breeding conditions, and offering opportunities for friendly contact with Jewish neighbors.

Marked differences were also found between the family conditions of the two age groups; but here it was the younger group (9 to 15) which was more favored.

The majority of children came from intact homes in which both parents were present. Half of the fathers were reasonably effective in their paternal roles. The relative soundness of the children's home backgrounds was reflected in their generally good school performance.

Of the youths (16 to 21), fewer had fathers who fulfilled their role; a good many came from broken homes, fatherless because of death, separation, alcoholism or illness. Not surprisingly, fewer of the youths than the children did well in school.

This distinction between the older and the younger boys parallels some findings reported earlier. As will be recalled, far more youths than children had delinquency records; and far more had been involved in plainly vindictive acts, as against wanton. The evidence concerning the older boys' homes would seem to suggest that anti-Semitic activity, in addition to other forms of delinquency, tends to occur more frequently where young people have been hurt by family disorganization; but it does not explain why this is so.

In the majority of cases, the surface appearance of the offender's backgrounds serves to underscore, rather than answer, our original question: If most of the culprits suffered no severe economic distress; if a great many had seemingly stable families; if their home neighborhoods did not breed delinquency; if their intelligence was average or higher—why, then, did they act as they did?

A clue emerges when the nature of the boys' offenses is read against their school achievement. The wanton mischief-makers, by and large, performed adequately in school, whereas the perpetrators of vindictive acts, though just as intelligent, were doing poorly. Unsatisfactory school work often signals the early stages of emotional disturbance; one might wish that the signal had been heeded. In any event, we must now examine the available evidence of emotional disturbance or deprivation among the boys.

The emotionally deprived

Apparently the court personnel handling the cases of these boys recognized, even on casual observation, that some might be suffering emotional disturbance. Seven out of 10 gang members and four out of five members of neighborhood cliques were referred by the courts for psychiatric examination. In contrast, most of the wanton vandals did not seem emotionally disturbed; only two of the five clique members and none of the play-group members were sent from the courtroom to the psychiatrist.

The reports of psychiatrists and social workers assigned to the cases referred for psychiatric study contain evidence of severe emotional deprivation or disturbance. Thus, one boy is described as "unable to cope with his increasing feelings of aggression" and "overwhelmed by intense sadistic impulses." These drives left him helpless as long as he was alone; he felt he could act them out only under the authority of a strong leader, and desperately sought the support of a group, in both acceptable and unlawful ways. He had little insight into his own behavior and saw nothing wrong with his swastika offense except having been caught.

Another boy felt actively rejected by his parents, Both father and mother held jobs and, according to the probation officer, both were so preoccupied with their ambition to move up the social ladder that the son was neglected. The mother reportedly displayed less emotion in talking about the boy than in describing her plans for a new home. The parents showed little concern about their son's offense; the only question that upset them was whether they would have to pay restitution.

A third youngster, aged 15½, was the oldest of seven children; both parents were employed—the father on two jobs—to support this large family. At school the boy did poorly in reading, arithmetic and social studies. Tests showed him to be depressed, withdrawn and greatly in need of acceptance. He habitually allied himself with a domineering friend from whom he could borrow strength; the clinical evaluation stated that he thought himself weak and others strong, and viewed all his social relationships in terms of power. The psychiatrist considered him potentially dangerous. Yet aparently he had received no significant help at school or through social agencies.

The youngster just mentioned disavowed anti-Semitic feeling, but his behavior indicated otherwise; in the course of an incident in which a Jewish child was molested, he had mimicked Jewish prayers. Unfortunately, this aspect of the case was not followed up by the court-appointed psychiatrist. That there was a family background of bigotry was revealed only when an interviewer for the present study found the father openly hostile to Jews.

The same failure to penetrate beyond individual psychology into the social problem of prejudice is found in most of the other cases. Personality tests employed did not include scales for measuring prejudiced attitudes. The anti-Jewish character of the offenses was usually disregarded, even where swastikas and anti-Semitic scrawls were in evidence. For the most part, psychiatrists and psychologists—as well as the social workers to whom the boys were assigned during probation—viewed their charges simply as recent delinquents, prompted by psychological needs or emotional problems within themselves or their families. That a larger problem—the role of society in sanctioning prejudice—was also involved does not seem to have been recognized by most of the clinicians or probation officers. Apparently there was little awareness that a violently anti-Semitic attitude might in itself call for clinical attention.

As far as they go, the case records are illuminating. They reveal an emotional deprivation as painful as bodily hunger and more dangerous to society. But they do not tell us why youngsters choose anti-Semitic symbols to express their feelings. Nor do they offer any reassurance that society possesses or is disposed to develop effective methods for identifying anti-social, aberrant behavior at an early stage.

Of the culprits apprehended in different parts of the country, some were found suffering from varying degrees of psychopathology. Five such offenders, all of whom had been referred by the courts for psychiatric examination or treatment, are described in the case histories below.

These histories, selected from a larger number, were obtained in various cities, independently of the study conducted by the Research Center of the New York School of Social Work. They are included here to supplement the findings of the study. Identifying details have been changed to protect the individuals ininvolved.

Jim F., a 15-year-old-boy in a community on the Eastern seaboard, was arrested as the organizer and leader of a neo-Nazi group which maintained a chemical laboratory for making explosives.

It was not Jim's first brush with the law. Four years earlier, he had been arrested for setting a false fire alarm, stealing a bicycle, attempting an auto theft and ransacking the glove compartments of cars. The judge released him with a warning, but a year later Jim and two friends broke into a school building to steal money and caused large-scale damage when they found none. The three boys, with Jim as leader, also broke into a community center, stole some property and set several small fires. Jim was now sent to a private training school for a year; he returned home apparently much improved, only to run away soon afterward. It was at this point that he organized the neo-Nazi group.

Jim is an intellectually superior boy, with an I.Q. of 138. At the observation center of the training school he was cooperative and got along well with others. He spent much time reading and showed an interest in many subjects. Although he called himself an atheist, he began to go to church after a few months, "for social reasons." He retained his feelings about naziism; while at the center, he talked much to the other boys about Hitler and Nazi beliefs, and attempted to start a "Nazi party."

Jim's parents were divorced when he was a year old; his mother remarried, but after nine years of conflict this marriage, too, ended in divorce. The mother, though interested in Jim's problems, was unable to cope with them; she felt intellectually inferior to her son.

Intensive testing and analysis yielded a diagnosis of schizoid personality, with a recommendation that Jim be referred for psychiatric treatment because of his pre-psychotic nature.

He received no such treatment. Instead, he was sent home and put on probation for an indefinite period. His latest anti-Semitic episode followed.

Carl P., a 16-year-old high-school boy living in a suburb of a Midwestern city, was arrested for painting swastikas on a high-school building and a Church. Although his behavior in school had been a severe problem for some time, he had had no previous contact with the courts.

Carl is intellectually superior, with an I.Q. of 132. At school he was an obsessive reader. An atheist, he read a great deal about religion, philosophy, anti-Semitism and the Nazis, took an interest in curious subjects—such as paganism and "God vs. Superman"—and wanted to free the world from religion. He belonged to a German club and for some time had been an adherent of Nazi philosophy.

The summer before his arrest, Carl learned that his parents had been divorced. They were married during World War II.

The father, who went overseas with the Army before Carl was born, neither returned to his wife after the war nor visited his son. The mother, a lifelong polio cripple, married again but this union, too, was unsuccessful; her second husband, an alcoholic, left the family several times during the marriage. Carl himself spent much of his early life with his grandparents, who leaned strongly toward anti-Semitic ideology. They lavished gifts on him and considered him a very gifted, "perfect" boy. While staying with the grandparents he saw his mother only intermittently.

After intensive analysis Carl was diagnosed as a psychotic with decided schizophrenic features. His swastika episode brought him to the attention of the authorities for the first time.

Fred H., aged 18, lives in a medium-sized city in the Southwest. We was arrested for painting swastikas on a local synagogue and on a museum in a nearby community; he had also set fire to a number of paintings in the museum.

Fred had loved to watch fires ever since childhood. When he was 12, he set a blaze under his house. He also was involved in other minor fires and, at the age of 16, came under suspicion of having taken part in a case of arson at a furniture store, but the police never established his connection with this incident.

Fred is the oldest of three children. His father, a skilled laborer, is described as ineffectual and immature, given to violent tantrums and, on occasion, physically aggressive toward his sons. The mother, although more intellectually inclined, also is immature and unstable. She has worked intermittently since the children were young, is a good housekeeper and stresses cleanliness.

Fred's early development was seemingly free of complications. He was a good athlete. As a small boy he became active in scouting and later rose to the rank of Eagle Scout; his mother was a Den Mother, his father a Scoutmaster.

At 16, Fred was extremely shy and withdrawn, spent much time reading at the library, played chess and listened to classical music. The parents separated for a short period, and Fred stayed with his father. Marked changes in his personality now became apparent. Referred to a child-guidance clinic, he refused to cooperate. He was then sent to a psychiatrist, who found him withdrawn and hostile, and made a diagnosis of schizoid personality, extremely disturbed. The psychiatrist recommended that Fred be given intensive treatment, and suggested that his parents also be referred for psychotherapy.

Four years before his arrest, Fred had become involved in an anti-Semitic organization, which met weekly. He helped distribute pamphlets and attended anti-Jewish meetings; he hated Jews, was also hostile toward Negroes and believed that the Germans were a superior race.

Committed by the court to a hospital, Fred was tested and found to be of superior intelligence. The diagnosis described him as a schizophrenic of paranoid type; indications for psychotherapy were considered poor.

The swastika episode for which he was apprehended revealed his prior history for the first time. Fred is now in a mental hospital in his home state.

Dick A., at 21, was committed for examination to a mental hospital in the Eastern community in which he lived. He was one of a few youths who sought to form a branch of the American Nazi Party, and to rally to its banner a group of young people who would wander through the country, spreading anti-Semitic propaganda.

Dick came from a broken home; his parents had separated when he was five years old and he saw his father only rarely. Upon reaching the second year of high school, he quit to join the Navy. Twice court-martialled for disorderly conduct and drunkenness, he subsequently received a medical discharge. He had been drinking heavily over a period of years; for this reason his relations with girls had invariably broken up. His drinking also lost him several jobs. He had not learned a trade.

About a year before his arrest, Dick saw a book display featuring The Scourge of the Swastika, a short history of Nazi war crimes by Lord Russell of Liverpool. He bought a copy of this work, which contains pictures of German atrocities. Two years earlier, he had picked up Hitler's Mein Kampf and become indoctrinated with the political meaning of the swastka. Reports of the Cologne desecrations inspired him to organize his neo-Nazi group; the members were later arrested for swastika offenses.

Dick's intelligence was normal. He was diagnosed as a schizoid personality, suffering from psychopathic personality disturbance and alcoholism. The examining court psychiatrist felt that the prognosis was uncertain, for Dick had shown serious maladjustment since adolescence and had taken up a dangerous social philosophy. Group therapy was recommended for him.

Afer being acquitted, Dick was discharged from the hospital to which he had been committed, with the recommendation that he attend a clinic for psychotherapy. Had it not been for his Nazi-like activities, he would not have come to the attention of the authorities.

Dan R., 15½, was brought before the children's court in a large Eastern city after breaking a window of a Jewish religious school.

Two years earlier Dan had come before this court for bicycle theft; he was put on probation and sent home. Some time later he was arraigned in the same court for stealing money from a neighbor's apartment, in company with two other boys. He was now sent to a hospital, for clinical and social analysis, but the analysis was not carried out and he was returned home. Within a few weeks, he stole several wallets from a neighbor's apartment and was charged with delinquency for the third time. On this occasion he was given a psychiatric examination by order of the court. Residential treatment was recommended and, pending disposition, he was committed to a youth center.

Dan's parents were intellectually limited people who had difficulty supporting their large family. Several of their eght children had been in children's court because of delinquency. The family structure was meager and the children received little parental supervision. Dan was markedly retarded in school. Though almost 16 years old, he read at the first-grade level; in arithmetic he did somewhat better. His behavior in the classroom made him hard to handle.

An intensive study revealed that, even though his performance was backward, Dan was well oriented, with a fair memory and intelligence in the low normal range. At the treatment center a diagnosis of schizophrenia, childhood type, was made. While at the center, Dan got along well with other youngsters and presented no behavior problems. Now that he has committed another offense, it remains to be seen what further treatment he will receive to prevent a recurrence.

The record of these five young people and others like them makes melancholy or even frightening reading. Not only was their own behavior pathological and anti-social; for the most part, they also proved themselves capable of leading others into anti-social acts.

Certain striking similarities are apparent in the case histories just presented. First, the majority of the boys were openly anti-Semitic, expressing their feelings both verbally and by the actions that brought them into court. Second, many were of superior intelligence, with I.Q.'s which, under different circumstances, would have enabled them to function as outstanding, responsible persons. Third, almost all came from homes with some degree of social disorganization—unhappy family relationships or separation of parents. And finally, in every instance the diagnosis was schizophrenia.

One may wonder, in each case, to what degree the psychological breakdown was induced by the boy's environment and to what degree by factors inherent in his personality—which remained undetected by the school, the family or the community. Despite superior natural endowments, the boys were poor learners and their behavior at school was uniformly provocative or troublesome. The crucial question therefore arises whether our school authorities and social mechanisms are sufficiently sensitive and alert to the dangers which may threaten a child when he is exposed to a combination of unfavorable circumstances and his character is not understood or wrongly interpreted. Suppose the illness had been detected and treated at the first sign of disturbed behavior or poor school performance—would the boys have needed anti-Semitism as an outlet for their personal and social difficulties?

It is not necessary to sympathize with arsonists and hoodlums; but we must reluctantly acknowledge that the youths involved in these cases might not have resorted to anti-social acts if help had been forthcoming in time. It is a depressing thought that society consistently failed these young people.

Cues and Incitements

Given the psychological predisposition, what precipitated the acts? Why did they occur when they did?

Many skilled observers suspected from the start that the main impetus was to be found in the wide publicity given the Cologne episode and those that followed. This assumption was confirmed in the interviews; again and again, the culprits said they got the idea from newspaper or television reports of these events.

Nazi Trappings and Models. Display of Nazi paraphernalia seems to have provided an additional stimulus. Salvaged from World War II, such gear had been sold for some time in Army-surplus stores, bookshops and "swap shops," presumably as "play material"—though one may ask if swastika armbands, helmets and gas masks are suitable playthings for children. Teen-agers paid as much as $70 for a uniform and helmet. During 1959, these outfits were occasionally seen in public, and pictures of the wearers appeared in some newspapers.

When asked where they had found their Nazi models, the teen-agers frequently mentioned books, movies and magazine stories about Hitler Germany, many of them strongly anti-Nazi in intent. Among the books, *The Scourge of the Swastika* was repeatedly named. A widely advertised phonograph record replete with Nazi martial music, entitled *Hitler's Inferno*, was also popular. These portrayals of the "virile Nazi" seemed to provide the strong-male image which so many of the boys lacked in their real lives.

Some of the younger boys modeled themselves on the older ones, copying misdeeds which teen-agers had bragged about. Even children obviously too young to know what it all meant sometimes took part in such imitative acts; two extreme cases, not included in the Research Center study, involved a child of five and another of six.

Social Influences. Social distance—a sense of mutual isolation —between Christians and Jews seems to have been an important factor in turning hostility against Jewish targets. True, many of the culprits lived and committed their offenses in districts with a high proportion of Jewish residents. But Christian and Jewish boys did not mingle. Proximity did not foster a sense of identification with Jewish neighbors or respect for their rights and property. An undercurrent of anti-Jewish feeling ran through these neighborhoods, including those that were outwardly stable. Though there might be no open fights, name-calling of Jews was common; Jewish children were frequently chased and synagogue windows broken.

Did anti-Semitism in the boys' families help to stimulate the acts? The parents nearly always denied any feelings of prejudice, but in interviews with probation officers or members of the study team they often mouthed the same anti-Semitic clichés voiced by their sons.

The young offenders seem to have been only slightly concerned about the reactions of adults living in the community. Though they did not want to be caught by the police and did not expect to be praised by their neighbors, they did not anticipate much criticism either. It is not surprising that prompt and stern censure of swastika outbreaks and their perpetrators by public officials, the clergy and other persons of high status did not deter these boys from further offenses. Pronouncements from such quarters rarely impress a young deviant; if anything, they confirm him in the belief that the world of organized society and public officialdom is not the world he wants for his own.

One might ponder a possible relationship between the boys' acts and the fact that they came from low-delinquency neighborhoods. We cannot rule out the possibility that they might have turned to ordinary delinquency instead of swastika daubing if the usual patterns of delinquent behavior had been much in evidence.

Why the Swastika? What did the swastika symbolize to the boys? Until the Cologne episode, many of them did not know what a swastika looked like or what it meant. Within two or three days after the initial outbreak, they gathered that it had something to do with Hitler, nazism and hatred of the Jews. They evidently chose it because its anti-Semitic character, as spot-lighted in the news media, appealed to their own anti-social impulses. During the weeks of mounting condemnation that followed, they must have learned that the symbol was socially unacceptable and likely to invite police action and punishment. This probably is the reason why most of the offenses covered by the study were committed surreptitiously, usually at night. Indeed, swastika incidents all over the nation followed this pattern; the culprits nearly always acted in the dark and often remained undetected.

Having appraised the effect of the various cues and incitements—news reports, the display of Nazi trappings, and local intergroup tensions—we must reluctantly conclude that most of the episodes were not meaningless mischief, but eruptions of latent anti-Semitism which persists in the American community. Usually buried and under control, this prejudice apparently can be precipitated into the open by factors such as those we have reviewed. Our conclusion is supported by the fact that offenses against Jewish targets still occur, though far less frequently. As this is being written, the desecration of a Jewish cemetery in New Jersey is reported. Red swastikas were painted on 41 tombstones; the damage is estimated at several thousand dollars. . . .

Close-up of a "Nazi" Group

Since the end of World War II, organized youth groups modeled on the Nazi pattern have occasionally sprung up in the United States. In recent years, only a few such organizations have come to public attention; these were found in widely separated parts of the country—in New York and California, Florida and Wisconsin.

Of the 13 groups included in the present study, two were essentially Nazi-oriented, rather than just incidentally tinged with Nazi-like behavior or symbolism. There is no evidence that they were part of a larger adult-directed organization; indeed, there is no indication from any source that adults had a hand in the 1959-1960 incidents in the United States.

The Research Center team was able to study one of the two Nazi-oriented groups in close detail, thanks to the cooperation of the Children's Court that heard the case.

The group under study was located in an urban area just outside New York City. Its membership consisted of boys between 10 and 15, all of whom had grown up together. Of 10 youngsters, apprehended, eight came from Irish-American families, one from a German-American family and one from a family of Scottish immigrants. Nine of the boys were Catholics; the religion of the tenth is not known. Six lacked one or both parents as a result of desertion, death or hospitalization for alcoholism or mental illness. Five went to parochial school and five to public school, but four of the latter had previously attended parochial school. All were intellectually normal, with I.Q.'s ranging from 93 to 114, but only six were doing well or even fairly well in school.

The group had taken shape gradually over two years; altogether, 20 or 30 boys had belonged at one time or another. Originally they occupied themselves with playing pirates and building crude underground clubhouses in vacant lots; but after several of these meeting places were wrecked by other boys, interest flagged.

It was at this juncture that one of the members, who later became a leader, bought a German helmet. Soon after this seemingly chance purchase, the whole group was collecting and wearing Nazi equipment: helmets, gas masks and insignia. There was an excitement in these belligerent trappings that turned the directionless group into a purposeful gang.

The boys now became more aggressive; they exercised regularly so as to be able to defend themselves against "the enemy" —other boys in the neighborhood—and on one occasion started a pointless fist fight with a Negro group. At the same time, they adopted a Nazi-style name and a formal organization with an authoritarian tone. A pledge, composed by the group and signed by each member, reads as follows (in the original spelling):

THE TEN COMMANDMENTS
OF A GERMAN (WHERMACHT) SOLDER

1. Never sourrender.
2. Be as nimble as a grey hound.
3. Keep your eyes and ears wide open.
4. Be as hard as drone steel.
5. No the full meaning of every attack, so that if your commanding officer is killed, you'll be able to carry it out yourself.
6. Never show mercy.
7. To you death must be a point of victory and honor to the 3rd Reisch of Germany.
8. Always show hard resistance.
9. Obey all orders.
10. No the ways and actions of the enemy.

For several months prior to the Cologne desecrations, members of the group painted swastikas around the housing project in which they lived; but these daubings provoked no public comment, nor were the daubers identified. What notice they attracted from adults during this period was not unfavorable; for example, the boys with their Nazi helmets and equipment once were photographed on a hike by passersby who apparently thought them amusing. The mother of one of the boys later asserted in court that she had been saddened when the group at first refused to admit her son.

During the winter of 1959-60, ten boys belonging to the group defaced synagogues and other buildings with painted swastikas. Indentified by a former fellow member, they were now apprehended by the police and referred to the probation department of the local Children's Court for investigation and supervision.

Two of the youngsters brought to court proved to be the ringleaders, five were loyal followers and three were casual hangers-on. Both leaders came from broken, severely disorganized homes, and under clinical examination both showed signs of personality distortion.

One of them, according to the psychological diagnosis, suffered from "an ego weakness severe enough to suggest that the boy borders on a schizophrenic development." The other was described as "a suppressed, anxious, sadistic boy who had found a mooring for himself in his identification with the Nazis." The diagnosis continued: "He is characterized by latent aggression and hate. He still needs a reason for expressing such a feeling, but his thinking is strange and often peculiar, and reality is often interpreted in distorted ways."

What attracted the two leaders to nazism was the apparent strength of the high-ranking Nazis and the supposed superiority of German military and scientific achievement; they overlooked the ultimate failure of the Nazis and the defeat of Germany.

Both leaders showed strong prejudice against Jews, as well as open antagonism against Negroes and Puerto Ricans. Long-standing anti-Semitism was also plainly voiced by several other members when asked their reasons for desecrating synagogues—although one of the more casual followers claimed to have participated merely to gain promotion to a higher rank, and another for fear of being called "chicken."

After its day in court, the group split into two fractions. One turned its attention to raising pigeons, riding horseback and other socially acceptable activities. The other remained stubbornly preoccupied with collecting Nazi gear; one of the former leaders, who now headed this faction, bitterly complained that the original collection remained impounded by the court.

The story of this group is a disturbing reminder of how emotionally unstable leaders can manipulate their followers into acts that lead inevitably to anti-social consequences. Again the question arises: Why did the community fail to perceive the danger while it was in the making?

Some Significant Findings

In examining the implications of the material here presented, we are guided by two basic thoughts.

First, young people who incline toward anti-Semitism are potentially dangerous, not only because any kind of bigotry is evil *per se*, but also because bigoted persons are open to manipulation by unscrupulous leaders.

Second, agencies working with children and youth, in such areas as social work, child guidance, recreation and education, should commit themselves to dealing with inter-group attitudes as an integral part of their practice.

The study findings most significant in this context may be summarized as follows:

Hostility against minority groups was found in varying degree in the backgrounds of the youngsters who were guilty of vindictive acts. Their homes, in many cases, were disorganized; their performance in school was frequently unsatisfactory.

The swagger and aggressiveness of typical delinquents were not evident. On the contrary, these boys were visibly beset by feelings of weakness and ineffectiveness, and leaned on tightly knit groups for support. Except where emotional illness was present, they were inclined to be secretive and to express their rebellion in devious ways; of the less sick, even the most anti-Semitic and sadistic could not assert themselves openly.

It is very important to recognize these warning signals early. Without timely intervention by teachers, school psychologists, educators or other professionals, it is all too likely that children of this type will grow into full-fledged anti-Semites. They may never become leaders of others, but their bigotry is likely to make them vulnerable to exploitation by demagogues later in life

For most of the younger offenders, the publicity given to the initial incidents seems to have supplied the chief incitement to overt misbehavior. To those whose families harbored anti-Semitic attitudes, the intensive coverage of the Cologne desecrations in newspapers and broadcasts evidently suggested a new way of expressing rebellion; in other words, where anti-Semitism was already in the background of the child, the fanfare of publicity fell on particularly receptive ears. To those of the older culprits who were previously involved in Nazi-like activities, the dramatic mass media accounts gave new encouragement.(11)

Sources of Social Tension

We know that some amount of anti-Semitism exists in some members of the population all the time, and there are always isolated instances of desecration, vandalism and intergroup hostility. (But) why should . . . the swastika incident in Cologne trigger a massive epidemic?

It seems as if the combination of predisposition and triggering incident must occur in a context of widespread social unease or tension if an epidemic is to result; or to put it another way, the small group of always willing participants must be augmented in some way, so that a large number of people who would otherwise not think of participating are drawn in.

There are a number of hypotheses about the social conditions which increase expressions of intergroup hostility. It has been suggested, for example, that where traditionally subordinate groups acquire symbols of economic wealth and prestige greater than those of the traditionally dominant group, the dominant group "as a whole, often resorts to terrorization to reassert the dogma of caste." Anti-Semitism in Nazi Germany has been seen as a response to the need for a "target for the discharge of the resentments arising from damaged self-esteem." An analysis of a race riot in Chicago argues that tensions there developed as the result of a rapid influx of Negroes into the city without adequate provision for their assimilation into the city's life so that relations between Negroes and whites "are marked by prejudice and competition, especially for jobs and housing."

All these hypotheses have in common the assumption that there has been a change in society of such a kind that two groups are either *realistically* in competition for some scarce commodity —such as jobs, prestige or housing—or that one group has suffered a loss in position, so that their security is threatened and they need someone to blame.

How do these hypotheses bear on our material? First, it is quite clear that the swastika epidemic appealed almost solely to one section of the population—adolescent boys. We are led to ask, then, about the kinds of pressures our society exerts on the high school youth which predispose him to this kind of hostile outburst. It is equally obvious, however, that not all high school boys participated in the outbreak, and those who did were not evenly distributed throughout the country. We must ask how the offenders differed from non-offenders in their social class, family background and personality type, and what local conditions in Phoenix, Levittown, Philadelphia or Los Angeles may have combined with these personal characteristics to produce participation. (Ed note: questions that were the precise lines of inquiry pursued by the American Jewish Committee study).

Furthermore, we must distinguish between sources of specific hostilities to Jews and sources of more diffuse hostilities which may be transferred to Jews. It may well be, for example, that in suburban areas where the Jewish middle class is growing, non-Jewish persons in the middle and lower middle classes are experiencing a threat to their self-esteem . . . In such a situation, parents may transmit their resentments to children—or children may be experiencing similar resentments in competition for scholastic or athletic honors.

More diffuse tensions may also result from social changes which do not explicitly involve competitive relations between Jews and non-Jews, however. The frustrated ambitions of working class youth, producing a generalized hostility to the adult middle class world, may be such a source of tensions. Or increased pressures on middle and lower middle class youth to achieve scholastic and social success in high school, to compete for increasingly difficult college entrance, may lead the adolescent to search for models of power and success with which he can identify. He may then turn to the neo-Nazi clubs and through them learn to direct his diffuse hostilities against Jews. In cases of such diffuse resentments, however, it is a matter of historical accident whether the target chosen is any one part of the population rather than another. . . .

The impact of the epidemic, and the publicity given to it, on the participants and potential participants must be evaluated apart from the impact on society as a whole. In some unknown proportion of cases, the swastika outbreak may well have given specific form and content to vague and diffuse hostilities, so that offenders who were not originally anti-Semitic have, in the course of the outbreak, learned about the prevalence—and for some, the legitimacy—of religious and ethnic intolerance. Their hostilities now have a new specific target. Others, however, who began with relatively mild and vague anti-Semitic sentiments, may well have been startled and abashed by the violent reaction their offenses provoked, learning that in this area at least, what seemed to them a legitimate and mild form of hostility is in fact a major transgression in the eyes of society. Just as the epidemic may have taught some to be anti-Semitic, it may have taught others not to be.(12)

BIGOT BUILDUP
CASE HISTORY OF GEORGE LINCOLN ROCKWELL

Organized bigotry, rabble-rousing and professional agitation of hate reached a highwater mark in the late thirties. Nazism in Germany combined with economic depression in this country to produce a native fascist and virulent anti-Semitic movement that was a major American social problem in the years prior to our entry into World War II. With the coming of war, the overtly subversive character of these groups forced them underground, to reappear at the old stand in the immediate post-war period. Post-war success was, however, short-lived. The relative prosperity of the country created an atmosphere hardly conducive to the screeds of the bigot-agitators. Additionally, they fell victim to a technique known as "quarantine treatment," an arrangement by which those who manage the mass media—radio, television, reputable newspapers and magazines—will avoid giving publicity to personalities whose only claim to public attention is their ability to provoke controversy by assailing racial and religious groups. In the absence of publicity—even negative and critical publicity—the agitator has difficulty reaching and extending his public.

During the fifties, although the extreme rightwing began to emerge as an identifiable political force in American life (see below, Section III, THE POLITICS OF PREJUDICE), overt anti-Semitism became increasingly unfashionable. In its quest for as broad a popular appeal as it could generate, the Right deliberately avoided being tarred with the brush of anti-Semitism. This was markedly true of the late Senator Joseph P. McCarthy and has continued to be true of the Birch Society—at least as far as official pronouncements and philosophy are concerned. (That followers of extreme conservative movements are frequently bigoted toward racial and religious minority groups is likewise a fact).

The deeply charged desegregation issue, however, gave a new impetus to the professional bigots. One such, George Lincoln Rockwell, self-styled leader of the American Nazi Party, represents a classic pattern of hate agitation. Utilizing "shock" technique to counter the effectiveness of "quarantine treatment," he has engendered publicity far out of proportion to either the strength or significance of his movement. He has himself given the cue to his efforts:

"All at once I had the answer! By being an OPEN, ARROGANT, ALL-OUT NAZI, not a sneaky Nazi—with the swastika, storm troops and open declaration of our intention to gas the Jew-traitors (after investigations, trials and convictions)—I would . . . make an end of this filthy silent treatment, for they could never ignore NAZIS with Swastika armbands and talk of gas chambers . . ."

The Anti-Defamation League in its issue of *Facts* (October, 1963) details the Rockwell story, including his catapult from obscurity to notoriety in just three years. The reader will also find interesting the indicated tie-in between Rockwell and the Black Muslims, Negro anti-white hate group.

In the Arlington, Virginia, headquarters of the American Nazi Party, there is a kind of shrine to Adolf Hitler. It is composed of a photograph of the Nazi dictator against the background of a large swastika flag, flanked by candles on each side. A swastika-shaped neon light hangs from the ceiling, and from it dangles a hangman's noose. A Jewish altar cloth is used as a doormat. Guns and ammunition are in evidence on the premises.

In this fall of 1963, George Lincoln Rockwell, leader of the American Nazi party, remains a nuisance, but is not a menace. Skilled performer though he is in achieving national notoriety. Rockwell has not been able to expand his movement and seems destined to remain a mere pimple on the American body politic. He could only become a real danger in an America struck by catastrophe and gone sick.

On the scene nearly eight years, Rockwell has in the last three or four years moved from one outrageous act to another as leader of the American Nazi Party, but has not found the formula that would expand or strengthen his "movement." No known important or respected person gives him support. The American people are not buying his message of hatred.

The annual "take" of the American Nazi Party is about $20,-000—derived mostly from small contributions and the sale of its published swill. Nevertheless, the "mileage" Rockwell gets from these limited returns in terms of news coverage alone is enough to make any press agent envious. And if he spends a little more than he takes in, Rockwell can make up the deficit, according to one of his storm troopers, by writing or visiting 20 people. Nevertheless, the Nazi fuehrer found it necessary, not long ago, to ask his troopers to find jobs and turn over their earnings to the party.

A Small Group

A recent head count showed 16 troopers in residence at Nazi Party headquarters in Arlington, Va., but how many of these flotsam and jetsam of American life saw fit to donate the proceeds of their labor to the cause is not a matter of record.

In the last two years, perhaps 50 other drifters have floated into the party headquarters, taken up residence in the barracks, stayed a while, and then moved on to greener and less gamey pastures. In all the United States, Rockwell may be able to muster another 25 or 30 uniformed troopers, the bulk of them clustered in small units of the ANP located in Chicago and Los Angeles. Rockwell's "front"—the Fighting American Nationalists —includes perhaps one or two hundred sympathizers scattered around the country.

Those who have dealt with Rockwell say the 45-year-old Commander has a fair share of leadership ability, imagination and verbal skill. Doubts have been raised as to his mental stability. Nevertheless, when Rockwell was committed to Washington's

St. Elizabeth's Hospital for observation, following a July 3, 1960, fracas in the nation's capital, two psychiatrists, according to The New York Times, found him "to be of sound mind and mentally competent to stand trial on a charge of disturbing the peace."

Headquarters, ANP

Headquarters of the American Nazi Party is a rickety two-story house in Arlington, Va. A second house nearby serves as a barracks. It is in these facilities that the members of the American Nazi Party—all two and a half dozen of them—operate on pseudo-military lines. Rockwell, of course, calls himself "Commander." His chief aides hold the rank of "Major." Down the line a bit further are "Captains" and "Lieutenants"—and at the bottom is the floating population of storm-troopers. Nazi uniforms and regalia are worn, and the troopers hold drills. They march to public meeting places in military formation. Part of their physical training consists of hitting a punching bag on which has been drawn a caricature of a Jew.

As part of the pseudo-military trappings, Rockwell holds party ceremonies at which awards, citations and medals are presented by the Commander to deserving subordinates. Breaches of party discipline, on the other hand, result in "courts-martial." (In April, Lt. Alan Welch received the "Medal of Merit" for "six months of hard work as Party Controller." Two Troop Leaders received the "Order of Adolf Hitler, Bronze Medal" for their "heroism and huge success in the 'Battle of Miami' in which they picketed the Anti-Defamation League and even invaded the Jews' 'sacred' Miami Beach to picket the starting rally for the rotten Jew Israel Bond Drive.")

But the life of a storm-trooper is not all action, glory and medals. Plumbing at headquarters is faulty, and hot water is in short supply. Troopers are often ordered to make necessary repairs since the Party Treasury cannot stand the strain of a regular plumber's services. The electrical system is likewise faulty and troopers must also make needed repairs.

The rest of the time, they hang around waiting for picketing assignments, work on the printing and publishing of party publications, organize teams to distribute leaflets, and sometimes accompany the Commander as personal bodyguards.

The rations are skimpy, unappetizing and monotonous. Some troopers have reported eating canned hash for days on end. At other times, the rations include cat food. At still other times, the diet has been a thin stew made from chicken necks.

The Commander has promised beefsteak when more money starts rolling in. He had hopes that this would come from sale of his autobiography, "This Time The World." The printing and binding of the book has had top priority among headquarters activities.

Rockwell's "Mein Kampf" runs 440 pages. It costs $10. A few hundred copies were printed and sold two years ago, some of them at $8 because the Party needed cash and offered a discount to stimulate quick sales.

The Commander had difficulty finding a printer to do the job. The job was finally done—laboriously—at Party headquarters in Arlington. A "front"—called Parliament House—was set up to provide a "publisher's" imprimatur.

The Commander announced grandiose plans to print "10,000 copies"—quite probably a highly inflated figure. In any event, troopers recently were still printing the book a page at a time, and busily gluing cloth to cardboard covers, and cutting up gauze to hold the pages together. Everything had to be done by hand. Everything moved at snail's pace.

A visitor to Party headquarters offered these impressions of an evening not too many months ago with the American Nazi Party:

Several troopers were discussing plans to picket the Jewish Community Center in Arlington. One trooper, a construction worker who rises at 5:30 a.m., looked tired and unhappy about the plan. The phones rang often. One California caller asked why literature he was expecting had not yet arrived. Other callers asked "foolish" question, or cursed the Nazis and hung up.

Upstairs, one trooper was working on mailing lists. He typed names and addresses on gummed stickers and stuck them on envelopes. The names were taken from a card file that contained, according to the visitor's guess, about 750 or 1,000 cards. The trooper complained about the Party's high postage bill.

Another trooper, estimating the cost of running the headquarters, put the figure somewhere between "hundreds of dollars' and $1,000 a week for expenses that included postage, Rockwell's trips, food, ink, materials for the printing press, paper, haircuts, cigarets, and the like. He said a "man in California" had recently come through with $500 to buy paper for Rockwell's book. The party was, as usual, behind in paying its telephone bill and fear was expressed that the phone company would remove the two phones in headquarters and the one in the barracks.

One trooper, fresh from Montgomery, Ala., arrived at headquarters. He had been sent to the Alabama capital to stir up trouble, but the police grabbed him when he arrived, reached into his pocket for money, and bought him a bus ticket, ordering him out of town.

Maj. Karl Allen, the Number 3 Nazi, arrived back at headquarters after visiting a jailed comrade cooling off in a cell a few hours from Arlington.

As work progressed during the evening, there was a noticeable atmosphere of unrest. Several troopers were bickering among themselves. Others, out of Rockwell's hearing—and later at a restaurant—complained about the Commander and his leadership of the Party. They resented his suggestion that troopers go to work and turn over their earnings to the Party.

They felt the Party was getting "too military." They felt that Rockwell was deliberately keeping the Party small to insure his continued personal control over it.

On other evenings, visitors might happen on a regular Party meeting and be exposed to a discussion of Hitler's "Mein Kampf," a study of the "Party Program", or a reading from the U.S. Constitution so that the troopers would know what was in it for them.

At all times, whether in private conversations at headquarters or in regular Party meetings, a major portion of everyone's time is consumed with repetitive condemnations of Communists, Jews, Negroes, and all others who oppose the Nazis.

A Look at the Record

Rockwell's headquarters is a hangout for criminals and vagrants. Some of those who congregate there have criminal records and a major percentage appear to have no visible means of support. Storm troopers and ex-troopers around the country have committed dozens of crimes.

A sampling of the year 1962 shows that Party members and sympathizers ran up this record of lawbreaking:

• On September 28, 1962, Roy James was convicted in Birmingham (Ala.) Recorder's Court of assault and battery and disorderly conduct in connection with an attack by him on Rev. Martin Luther King. James received a 30-day jail term and a $25 fine. Later, at a ceremony at ANP headquarters in Arlington, James was awarded a medal for his "gallant action" in Birmingham.

• On July 19, 1962, Roger Foss and Gene Shalander were convicted in Miami City Court on charges of vagrancy and disorderly conduct. In addition, Foss was found guilty of attacking a policeman. He was sentenced to 180 days and a $500 fine, or 60 additional days. Shalander was sentenced to 120 days and a $500 fine, or 60 additional days. The episode was somewhat less "sensational" than the headlines Foss made back in August, 1960, when he disclosed that the First Secretary of the Soviet Embassy had paid him $500 "to infiltrate the government and society." A few days after Foss made the revelation in 1960, the U.S. Government ordered the Soviet official expelled. Rockwell praised Foss for his patriotism in reporting the Soviet offer to the FBI—and made Foss the "hero" of the hour. (The ANP's "Intra-Party Confidential Newsletter" of April 16, 1963 reported the resignation of Lt. Roger Foss and described him as "one of the most able and well-liked Nazis at National Headquarters." It was Foss second resignation from the Party).

• On February 14, 1962, Schuyler Ferris forfeited collateral in Washington, D.C. on a charge of disorderly conduct. He had refused to obey a police order directing him to leave a theater lobby.

• On April 12, 1962, Karl Allen and Bernard Davids were convicted of disorderly conduct in Washington, D.C., Municipal Court, and were sentenced to ten days in jail. They had trampled a Soviet flag.

• On August 9, 1962, Lawrence Smith forfeited $10 in connection with a disorderly conduct charge that was lodged against him after he had handcuffed himself to a gate of the British Embassy in Washington, D.C.

• On September 22, 1962, seven Nazi storm troopers forfeited collateral in Washington, D.C. after they were charged with disorderly conduct for fighting in front of the White House.

• On September 29, 1962, Harry Blair was convicted in Baltimore Municipal Court of unprovoked assault on Charles Bowling, a Negro. He was sentenced to one year in the Maryland House of Correction. On the same day, Blair and Weston Weed were convicted on charges of disorderly conduct and were sentenced to 60 days in the city jail. (Weed made headlines a few months later when, police said, he stole a total of $30,000 from several supermarkets in his home town of Moorestown, N.J. and claimed he had turned over some of the money to the ANP. Rockwell denied receiving such a "gift.")

• On June 21, 1962, Eugene Lambert, Clifford Uthene and Wayne Mueller of the Chicago branch of the ANP were convicted in Chicago's Jury Court of criminal defamation and disorderly conduct. Lambert and Uthene were sentenced to one year jail terms and were fined $700 each. Mueller drew four months and a $300 fine.

The record for 1963 is not very different—is, if anything, worse. Nazi Party members have been involved in street fighting in Miami, Los Angeles and right in front of party headquarters in Arlington, Va. One member was arrested on charges of possessing a gun, which was a violation of law in his case because he was a convicted felon. One of the troopers who went to jail in Miami in 1962—Gene Shalander—is sought on a charge of deserting his wife and two small children. Mrs. Shalander told a newspaper that her husband felt the payment of money for the support of his children was, in his words, "blood money."

In the Streets

Of all the tactics employed by Rockwell, the use of shock techniques and outrageous acts, aimed at forcing the public to pay attention to his antics, has probably been the most effective from his viewpoint. Since Rockwell's organization appeared on the scene, its street tactics—some might call them gutter tactics —have produced most of its publicity and notoriety.

At first, most of the "action" consisted of handing out inflammatory and provocative literature on the streets of Washington, D.C. Then in 1960, there were Sunday afternoon party "rallies" on the Mall—and elsewhere—in Washington which resulted in several disorders. Later, there were picket lines.

The technique used by Rockwell for any public "action" tends to follow a pattern. Some days before the scheduled demonstration, Rockwell or other Party leaders notify the local press, radio and television media. A day before the action—or on the same day—they phone the local police and the FBI to ask for protection against the very people whom they plan to provoke.

Early in 1961, the Nazis carried out a series of picketing demonstrations when the motion picture "Exodus" was premiered in various cities. Demonstrations were held in Boston on January 15th, in Philadelphia on Febraury 1st, in Detroit on February 11th, in Washington on February 20th, and in New Orleans on May 24th. At the same time, frequent distributions of party literature were being staged on the streets of Washington.

The Boston, Philadelphia and New Orleans actions prompted by the premieres of "Exodus" were important events for Rockwell and his followers. They were heavily publicized by the information media. They turned parts of great cities upside down. And they stimulated a flow of contributions to the Nazi Party from sympathizers scattered around the country.

In Boston, where Rockwell received substantial advance publicity, thousands of angry citizens descended on downtown streets, near the theater where "Exodus" was being screened. When Rockwell and two troopers appeared, and the crowd spotted their Nazi regalia and armbands, the Nazis were showered with eggs and stones. Some tried to punch Rockwell and his aides. Only quick action by a specially-trained unit of the Boston police saved Rockwell and his henchmen from a bad beating— or worse. Rockwell, considerably shaken, was taken into "protective custody", escorted to the airport, and seen on to a plane. Meanwhile, police intercepted a truckload of late-arriving troopeers from out-of-state, and escorted them back to the State Line.

In Philadelphia, two weeks later, Rockwell himself stayed behind, but sent three of his men to picket "Exodus" at a downtown theater. Only one of the three pickets was dressed in Nazi uniform. Nevertheless, thousands of enraged Philadelphians rushed the Nazi pickets, and again quick police work prevented the Nazis from being beaten.

Although the picketing action was abortive, the mere presence of the three Nazis triggered a near-riot in "The City of Brotherly Love" which ended with the arrest of the three Nazis and 64 anti-Nazi Philadelphians.

In May, 1961, when the "Freedom Riders" were making headlines around the country, Rockwell sought to get into the act, and milk new notoriety from national interest in the Southern situation. He conceived the idea of a "Hate Bus"—a Volkswagon festooned with anti-Negro and anti-Jewish slogans—to drive southward from Washington, using the same general route taken by the Freedom Riders earlier, and trailing publicity in every city and hamlet along the way.

When the "Hate Bus" reached the outskirts of New Orleans, police ordered the crew of troopers manning the bus to remove the anti-Negro and anti-Jewish signs. Rockwell meanwhile, flew into New Orleans to lead his troopers in picketing "Exodus" and a rally of the NAACP scheduled about the same time. On May 24th, Rockwell and nine followers, some in full uniform, some wearing armbands but regular street clothes, attempted to picket the movie. As soon as they raised their picket signs, police arrested them, fearing possible violence because almost two hundred angry citizens had gathered outside the theater.

The Nazis, including the Commander himself, were charged with "disturbing the peace by unreasonably alarming the public." Aping the "Freedom Riders", the Nazis went on a hunger strike while in jail. They were found guilty and fined, but a year later, the Criminal District Court of Appeals reversed the convictions, declaring that the "attire of the defendants and the offensive nature of the slogans did not involve a violation of law." Again, the payoff to Rockwell and his Nazis came in the form of press notoriety achieved by their provocative behavior and slogans.

During 1962, Nazi street actions took place at the White House in Washington, at the Washington, D.C. headquarters of the Democratic National Committee, at Anti-Defamation League offices in Miami and Philadelphia, and at the Jewish Community Building, in Los Angeles. Rockwell's men were most successful in roiling the atmosphere of Philadelphia.

There, on June 26th, an angry crowd of 500 Philadelphians put a quick end to an attempted picketing of the ADL office by six Nazi troopers, several of them from out of town. The pickets bore placards shrieking "Gas The Traitors" and the crowd quickly tore the signs to bits, shouting "Kill the Nazi bastards". As police moved in to try to take the pickets into protective custody, the crowd broke through police lines, and a full-fledged riot developed. When it was over, a number of those involved needed medical attention. No charges were lodged against the Nazis, but the non-Philadelphians who picketed were escorted to the city line by the police.

On October 12, 1962, five Nazis set out to picket a meeting featuring Communist leader Gus Hall as the main speaker and scheduled for the Adelphia Hotel. Announcement of the Nazis' intentions received publicity in local papers, and on radio and TV.

As the Nazis arrived at the Adelphia Hotel, and started to get out of their cars, a waiting crowd fell upon them, a fracas ensued, police and civilians were injured, and the five Nazis arrested and fined.

The street fights and near-riots continued into 1963. In Miami, on March 2nd, two Nazis wearing the swastika armband and Nazi-type jackboots set off a near-riot outside the Fontainebleau Hotel, where a banquet for the Israel Bond campaign was scheduled. The Nazis carried signs and placards on which had been emblazoned, in red: "Zionism is Treason", "Death to U.S. Traitors", "Buy U.S. Bonds, Not Israel Bonds", and "Forget Israel, Free Cuba." A group of 12 or 15 cab drivers and carhops rushed toward the Nazis, forcing the police to move swiftly and to take the Nazis into protective custody.

In Los Angeles on April 14, 1963, four Nazis picketed a march by members of "Women Strike for Peace" and 1000 college students. The Nazis were spat upon, and were hit by garbage and by eggs. (Picketing the Peace march, independent of the Nazis, were members of the John Birch Society).

Two weeks later, also in Los Angeles, five Nazis came prepared for trouble they sought to provoke by picketing at the Shrine Auditorium, where a ceremony marking Israel's 15th Anniversary was being held. All five Nazis were in uniform. Three of the five wore brown steel helmets, which they had learned to use as weapons. All carried four-foot clubs to which had been attached signs bearing anti-Jewish slogans. Shouting "Kill the Jews!" the Nazis bulled their way into the crowd waiting to get into the auditorium.

The Los Angeles Herald Examiner later reported: "Almost immediately there was hissing, booing and spitting by the Nazis and onlookers. Obviously by prearrangement, witnesses said, the Nazi toughs tore off their placards and started swinging wildly at everyone within reach of their clubs."

A major riot call was issued and police responded. The Nazis

were subdued. Three policemen and six civilians were injured.
The Nazis were charged with conspiracy and assault with deadly
weapons.

In each case, however, Rockwell reaped newspaper notoriety
from the street action of his Nazi Party toughs.

On the Campus

If Rockwell has received some of the press notoriety he craves
as the result of street action by the drifters and vagrants he calls
storm troopers, he has also received publicity from speaking appearances—during 1962 and 1963—at American colleges and universities. Apparently these appearances, and the resulting press
notices, have served as an important morale booster for the Nazi
Party Commander. Even when an invitation is cancelled, as has
been the case at the University of Pittsburgh, at Bucknell, at
Northwestern, and at the University of Illinois, Rockwell gets
headlines, controversies over so-called "freedom of speech" are
carried on in newspaper editorials, in campus publications and in
letters to the editor, and the Nazi Party is a center of attention
and discussion for a brief interlude.

If Rockwell speaks there is a hub-bub of controversy. If he is
banned, there is also a hub-bub of controversy. Once a student
group invites him, whether out of curiosity or out of a somewhat
distorted notion of what constitutes free speech, Rockwell cannot lose in terms of publicity and attention. He knows this. He
plays on it.

His actual college appearances, however, are less rewarding
to him than the controversy caused by invitations to speak. Rockwell has usually tried to tone down the blatant bigotry and violent Nazi philosophy that suffuses him and his movement and
to adopt a pseudo-academic pose in outlining his views. Because
university officials insist, he doffs his uniform, appears in civvies.
He carries an attache case. But he is still Rockwell. And he
rarely fools the student audiences. He has been hooted, jeered
and booed—but he has also been listened to attentively. American college students are either inherently polite or surprisingly
curious.

Rockwell has drawn fairly large audiences. He has provoked
controversy and some disorder. At San Diego State College in
California on March 8, 1962, he drew a good crowd and made
headlines across the country when a Jewish student was provoked into leaping toward the rostrum and taking a punch at the
Nazi Commander.

At Carleton College, Northfield, Minn., more than 1000 students turned out to hear him and the newspapers in nearby

Minneapolis and St. Paul featured his appearance in front-page stories, while TV stations interviewed him on his arrival.

At the University of Chicago on February 25, 1963, Rockwell spoke to 300 students, while hundreds of others were turned away because the hall could not hold them. Before he arrived, the campus newspaper commented editorially that he was more likely to gain publicity than converts. Rockwell's tone was restrained, his wisecracks sharp. Some students expressed surprise that they had not heard a lunatic. It was, altogether, a successful evening for Rockwell.

His appearance the following evening at Shimer College, Mt. Carroll, Ill., was, however, a flop. Shimer is a 250-student experimental school, affiliated with the University of Chicago. Unfortunately for the Commander, some of his historical allusions were garbled and inaccurate. The academic pose was shattered. Students began walking out on him during his talk. An eyewitness said that those who remained constantly interrupted his remarks with derisive laughter.

It was not the first time the Commander had underestimated the high standards of college audiences. At the beautiful campus of the University of Virginia on February 14, 1963, Rockwell had been invited to speak by the conservative John Randolph Society, a small debating group which a week earlier had offered its platform to Communist leader Gus Hall. The invitations to Hall and Rockwell had produced a furor throughout the Old Dominion. The Governor, the newspapers and the American Legion were involved in the public debate, and the Richmond Times-Dispatch suggested that students stay away from the talks "in droves."

The student newspaper took issue with the Times-Dispatch. "We shall go hear the speakers," it said editorially. "We will not hide from their propaganda . . . We do not believe that the values which have sustained us for so many years will be seriously challenged in an hour."

When Rockwell appeared, he was dressed in sober and conservative garb. He opened his remarks in pseudo-intellectual fashion and then, mistaking the traditional gentlemanliness and politeness of the audience for sympathy toward him and his views, became wilder and wilder in his statements. First the audience laughed. Then it booed. Then it hissed. After the "lecture" ended, students—openly critical—commented that among other distasteful aspects of the evening, Rockwell's storm troopers, who had accompanied him, looked "hoody" and "like thugs."

In March, 1963, Rockwell talked via telephone to a study group at Central Missouri State College in Warrensburg, and on April 26th, he spoke to a journalism class of 28 at the University of Maryland. In May, he was invited—then "disinvited"—by a student group at the University of Massachusetts.

On May 14, 1963, while on trip to the West, he spoke at the University of Colorado in Boulder. Perhaps the highlight of the event was that his audience totalled 3000 students.

In almost every case where Rockwell spoke on the campus of an American institution of higher learning, a student group—usually a small one—had invited him. In one case—the University of Pittsburgh—a Rockwell aide sought the invitation but college authorities vetoed the idea. Why had student groups invited him?

There were various explanations. Some student leaders said they wanted a dramatic personality who could fill a hall and provide an evening's diversion. Others were merely curious. Still others were intrigued by the daring act of inviting a Nazi to appear. A few thought the Nazis represented "one side" of important issues and professed to see in the Nazi "program" something worthy of serious discussion. Finally, some felt that by inviting Rockwell they were showing their faith in "free speech."

On net balance, Rockwell's sortie into the college "lecturing" arena has probably done him little harm and most likely a little good. If he has been laughed at on most appearances, he helped his "image" at the University of Chicago. But most of all, whenever he was invited, whether he eventually appeared or not, he was the center of attention and controversy, he reaped pages of press notices, and achieved the notoriety which he has consciously set out to stimulate by most of his public activities.

Materials For Sale

Rockwell writes profusely and what his bombastic prose may lack in quality is somewhat offset by the sheer volume of verbiage he spews forth. His level of literacy and his literary "talent" appears to be several cuts higher than that of the drifters and stumblebums in his "elite" corps. Nevertheless, his group of vagrants form a valuable auxiliary for outpourings of the Commander. They cut paper, run the mimeograph machine and the printing press, and they staple pages and address envelopes.

But it is the Commander who carries the ball, and he has some know-how when it comes to preparing lurid artwork, planning layouts, and dreaming up inflammatory and provocative headlines.

As noted, Rockwell's autobiography—"This Time the World"—first made its appearance two years ago. Here's how Rockwell, himself described it: "The inspiring story of the rise of the U.S.

Nazi Party. A damning expose of the Jew-Communist-Zionist-Race-mixing conspiracy and complete plans for victory by White Christian Americans. Hundreds of photos of German and American Nazis, fights, riots, speeches, arrests, etc. First edition sold out! Autographed upon request."

Some of the publications available from Arlington bore such titles as: "Niggers! You Too Can Be A Jew!"; "Communism Is Irish!"; "Proof That Goldwater Is A Plant!"; "Eichmann Speaks!" Also offered for sale were assorted swastika gummed-stickers bearing such slogans as "Hitler Was Right!!!" Other items included official ANP swastika armbands ("for souvenir purposes only") as well as photos of Hitler, the late Senator McCarthy and Commander Rockwell.

At the end of March, 1963, Rockwell's mimeograph began grinding out a new weekly publication of three or four pages, bearing the title of "Intra-Party CONFIDENTIAL NEWSLETTER." The opening paragraph of the first issue said the new publication was "a TOP SECRET, intra-party communique and will be sent only to active Associate Members, Party units, affiliates and a very select number of supporters." And it added: "It is to be kept in a locked place or burned."

The "top-secret" hush-hush document carries drafted routine announcements of Party activities in various localities, reports awards to members, as well as transfers and resignations. It urges readers to send in news of Party activity and to subscribe to Jewish newspapers for party purposes. Readers are also urged to contribute postage stamps to help ease the drain on the party treasury made necessary by mailing costs.

Of all the publications which have been turned out at the Nazi headquarters in Arlington, the sickest and the most sickening is a little picture booklet called "The Diary of Ann Fink." It contains 16 pages of the most sordid photos of Hitler's concentration and extermination camps and the walking skeletons victimized by Hitler—with captions supplied by the Commander or his henchmen.

Beneath each picture of human misery is an example of American Nazi Party "humor." One photo shows a human corpse half inside a concentration camp oven. The caption: "I asked for a cheap pad . . . But this is ridiculous." Another photo shows one of the "walking dead"—an emaciated skeleton with protruding ribs and the bulging eyes of the near rear staring from a face that can only be described as a skull. He is being supported by a sturdier man at the time of the Liberation in World War II. The caption: "How many times does your old coach have to tell you . . . Give up smoking or you'll never be a champion."

The two-page center-fold contains a photo of a human being, clinging to a barbed-wire fence, half-lying, half-sitting, his head bowed and apparently half-dead. The caption: "Man-o-manoshewitz, what a wine!"

Rockwell and the Black Muslims

At first glance, one of the strangest phenomena on the American scene is the courtship of the Black Muslims by George Rockwell, a racist Nazi. The incongruity is, however, merely superficial for in essence, both the Muslims and the Nazis share a common viewpoint on what the relationship between the white and Negro people ought to be. They both believe in complete separation.

The Muslim movement—a pseudo-Islamic sect that is tough, disciplined and uncompromising—believes that Negroes can expect nothing good from whites, whom they describe as "white devils," and that the only answer is complete "apartheid." They seek establishment of an all-Negro nation within U.S. borders, or a return to Africa—but in any event, one of their slogans is "land of our own."

Rockwell, who has described American Negroes as "the lowest scum of humanity" and as "half-ape, Congo cannibals transplanted to America," has his own plans for the Negro should the day ever come when he controls the destinies of the United States. He proposes to ship American Negroes to Africa and claims that millions of Negroes want to go there.

While Rockwell claims that neither he nor the Nazis "hate" Negroes—"any more than we hate our children or servants or dogs because they are our inferiors mentally"—he still would get rid of them. "We propose," Rockwell wrote in the "Trooper's Manual," "to . . . make their African homeland so attractive and decent for them that only a damned fool would rather stay here and try to force his way to acceptance rather than lead his own 'dark' continent with his American know-how and our sincere and generous help."

Should any "die-hard" or "uppity" American Negroes insist on remaining in their native land "where they are not wanted," the Nazi leader—if he had power—would "repeal the amendment to the Constitution which makes these Africans into 'Americans' —an impossibility as absurd as to pass a law to make 'Chinamen' out of Negroes, just because they happen to live in China."

In the Black Muslins, Rockwell sees a Negro leadership and a Negro force whose aims appear to dovetail with his own, and so he has found it possible to record some extremely laudatory sentiments about them:

"From out of the rotten ranks of the lowest scum of humanity—the half-ape, Congo cannibals transplanted to America—rose two incredible men with an ability for leadership which can only be seen as miraculous in view of the utter failure of these people to produce anything but savages and slaves for hundreds of thousands of years. Out of the unspeakable black gheetos (sic) of America; out of the dope, filth, prostitution, dice games, razor fights and utter degradation of black America rose two men of truly heroic proportion—Elijah Muhamed (sic) and Malcolm X."

Elijah Muhammad is the aging and ailing leader of the Black Muslims, and Malcolm X—an articulate ex-convict of tremendous energy and organizing ability—is sometimes described as Elijah's heir apparent, and always as the "Number Two Man" of the Muslim movement.

At the Muslim's annual convention in Chicago on February 25, 1962, Rockwell was one of the speakers before an audience of 5,000. Although some in the audience booed when Rockwell rose to speak, he ignored the manifestation and declared:

"I am proud to stand here before black men. I believe Elijah Muhammad is the Adolf Hitler of the black man."

Eyewitnesses reported that Mr. Muhammad and Malcolm X applauded Rockwell's statement. So did some in the audience. Others booed again.

But then Rockwell took off on the Jews, charging that the Jews were "exploiting your people and my people" and asked the audience whether Negro organizations needed Jewish leadership. He received a resounding "no" from the assembled Muslims.

At the end of his speech before the convention, Rockwell gave the Nazi salute and shouted "Heil Hitler." The handful of storm-troopers with him stood up and also saluted. Again, many in the audience booed.

During Rockwell's speech, however, observers noted that Muhammad and his top aides applauded the Nazi leader enthusiastically and that the audience did so when he praised Muhammad. But the same listeners booed his expressions of admiration for Hitler and many of them, obviously shocked by Rockwell, grumbled to their neighbors about his presence and some of his remarks. At one point, a group of young men in the balcony of the auditorium shouted at Rockwell: "Sit down and shut up!"

Rockwell's speech at the 1962 Muslim convention was not the first time he had appeared at such a gathering. At Washington's Uline Arena, where a Muslim rally attended by 7,000 was held on June 26, Rockwell sat in the front row with 20 of his troopers. As Malcolm X strove mightily to extract every loose dollar from the faithful, who had been brought to Washington from around the country in 100 chartered buses, the Washington Star reported that "a shrill voice called out from the audience:

"George Lincoln Rockwell gives twenty dollars. He was applauded . . .
Malcolm X said: 'George Lincoln Rockwell, you got the biggest hand you
ever got, didn't you?'"

Again, on May 7, 1963, Rockwell went out of his way to demonstrate his "affinity" for the Muslims. He was in Los Angeles
on "party business"—the scheduled trial of the five Nazi troopers
who had staged a near riot at the Shrine Auditorium on the
occasion of Israel's 15th anniversary. But when the trial was
delayed two weeks, the Commander marched himself down the
corridor to the courtroom where a long line had formed for the
trial of 14 Muslims, charged with assault and interfering with
the police in a riot outside the Los Angeles Mosque of the Black
Muslims on April 27th. In the disorder, one Muslim had been
killed by police bullets, another was paralyzed for life, and five
others were wounded. The Black Muslim movement was enraged.

The riot—and the indictment and trial of the Muslims—made
headlines in Los Angeles, and Rockwell's appearance at the
courtroom was a golden opportunity to cash in on the press and
public interest in the trial. He did not let it pass.

A Los Angeles newspaper reporter described the scene outside —the courtroom as follows:

"He greeted several Muslim leaders in friendly fashion and received
cordial—if somewhat astonished—replies. 'The Muslims,' he said, 'are
being persecuted just as the Nazis are being persecuted. They are dedicated to the same ideals as the Nazi Party—the separation of the black and
white races—and we work together in many things.'" (The Black Muslim
leadership has never commented publicly on whether it actually "works
with" Rockwell).

Having set the tone for his remarks, Rockwell became expan-
sive.

"The fact is," he declared, "that most of the Negro people in
this country are in complete agreement with the Muslims and
their ideals just as most of the white people in this country are in
agreement with the Nazis. The only job before us to remove
their fear and set them free to join us . . ."

As to the trial of the Muslims, Rockwell declared that they
were not getting a fair trial and that they would be "railroaded
for crimes they did not commit, just as my own boys are being
railroaded over the trouble at the Israel rally."

(On June 14, 1963, an all-white jury found eleven Muslims
guilty, acquitted two defendants, and disagreed on one defend-
ant.)

Whether Rockwell's professions of common purpose with
respect to the Black Muslims, and his appearances at Muslim

gatherings and scenes of crisis, represent a sincerely-held view that his goals of "back to Africa" and apartheid are consonant with those of Muhammad's movement, or whether he has merely sought to cash in on the extraordinary amount of press coverage the Muslims have received—or both—are questions whose answers lie hidden deep in the recesses of the Commander's turbulent brain.

But his "courtship" of the Muslims is—as has been noted—a matter of record.

Hate, International

At the end of July, 1962, Commander Rockwell left the United States to attend an August meeting of the British National Socialist Movement, headed by British Nazi Colin Jordan. Rockwell and Jordan, who had maintained a correspondence, had dreamed up a grandiose plan for the establishment of a World Union of National Socialists—an international Nazi organization which would weld small clumps of like-minded admirers of Adolf Hitler in various countries into a solid phalanx.

Apparently anticipating the opposition of the British Government to his entering the United Kingdom, Rockwell flew first to Shannon Airport, in the Irish Republic, and from there made his way to Britain. There is no immigration check between Ireland and Britain. On August 3, 1962, the British Government announced that Rockwell would not be allowed to enter the country to attend.

Much to the later embarrassment of British authorities, Rockwell was already in England at the time the announcement was made—having secretly been spirited into the country by Jordan's Nazis, who had made elaborate arrangements for the task.

The meeting to set up the international Nazi organization was held at Dead-and-Bury Hollow, in Guiting Wood, near Cheltenham, about 130 miles west of London. It was a stormy affair. The Nazis assaulted news photographers who tried to take pictures, and chased off newspaper reporters. Finally, however, enraged villagers near the Nazi encampment invaded the meeting and broke it up, destroying the camp as well.

Nevertheless, out of the meetings came a ringing manifesto that made up in bombast what it lacked in reality. Rockwell claimed it was written in a tent under "combat conditions." It was called the "First Working Draught of The Cotswold Agreement Between the National Socialist Delegates of Great Britain, the United States, Germany, Austria, France, the Irish Republic and Belgium Assembled in International Convention in the Encampment in the Cotswold, United Kingdom"—"The Cotswold Agreements" for short. The document formally established a so-called "World Union of National Socialists" (or "WUNS") with Jordan as International Leader Pro Tem. Rockwell was named as Deputy.

It vowed war on "the international Jewish Communist and Zionist apparatus of treason and subversion" through a "monolithic, combat-efficient, international political apparatus." But that was not all. Part of the grandiose scheme was "to work toward the unity of all White People in a National Socialist World order," as well as toward "suitable arrangements with non-white leaders of other races to advance racial dignity and justice for each race on the basis of total and absolute geographic separation of the races." In addition to this plan for world "apartheid," the Nazi "summit meeting" agreed "to work for just allocations of suitable and reasonable portions of the earth's surface for the exclusive sovereignty of the Black Race, of the Yellow Race, of the Red Race, and of the Brown Race," and to "work toward an eventual world ORDER based on RACE, with just representation from each RACIAL group." Finally, the Nazis resolved to take up where—presumably—Eichmann had left off and "to find and accomplish on a world-wide scale a just and final settlement of the Jewish problem."

Having agreed—in their first eight sentences—to carve up the globe on the basis of race, the handful of Nazis who gathered in England in the summer of 1962 went on to spell out— in the turgid prose from which they seem unable to refrain—the details of their new "world organization." It was to be a union of Nazi groups acknowledging the "spiritual leadership" of Adolf Hitler. Only one Nazi group was to be admitted from any single country. Pending "the World Nazi Congress of 1963" individuals would be admitted from countries where no Nazi group had yet signed the Cotswold Agreements, but in no case would an individual be admitted to membership as long as there was a WUNS signatory group in his country.

The provision for admission of individuals may well be taken as evidence of the miniscule strength of the international Nazi movement, just as the proposed slicing up of the planet Earth may be taken as evidence of the unreal, never-never land in which the leaders of the Nazi movement mentally dwell.

After the 1962 gathering at Dead-and-Bury Hollow, Rockwell, again disappearing, played hide-and-seek for days with the Special Branch of Scotland Yard, as British newspapers reported him seen in various parts of the British Isles. Finally, on August 9th, the British Government deported Rockwell as an undesirable alien.

Permanent leaders of the WUNS were to be chosen at the World Nazi Congress of 1963, but the year is almost out and the Congress has not yet been held. It is unlikely that it will be held.

For events moved rapidly after the 1962 gathering in England. Following Rockwell's deportation, the British Government moved swiftly against Jordan and his organization. On Oct. 2, 1962, Jordan and three other leaders of "Spearhead"—military arm of the British Nazi organization—went on trial in London's Old Bailey.

Charged with organizing, training and equipping the "Spearhead" group for the use of physical force for political purposes, Jordan and his lieutenants were found guilty on two of four counts, and on October 15, 1962, were sentenced to jail terms, Jordan drawing nine months, one of his henchman six months, and the other two three months apiece.

Rockwell, as Deputy Leader Pro Tem of the WUNS, assumed command when this tragedy befell the international Nazi "movement." And nothing has been heard of the WUNS since.

Rockwell made a brief sortie into Canada by auto in August, 1962—shortly after his return from England—to seek out a "fuehrer" for a Canadian Nazi party, but while he was looking for a likely prospect, the Montreal hotel where he was staying discovered his true identity, and he was evicted as an "undesirable person." As if this indignity were not enough, the Commander was barred from again entering Canada by the Canadian Government.

In October, 1962, while Jordan and the other British Nazis were on trial, Rockwell wrote the Argentine National Socialist Front, asking for information about a Nazi-type organization called "Tacuara"—which was making headlines by perpetrating anti-Jewish acts of violence. Rockwell also asked what the Argentine Nazi comrades thought of holding "our World Nazi Congress of 1963 in Argentina." The reply he received is lost to history, but on January 20, 1963, a spokesman for the Argentine Embassy in Washington said that Rockwell had applied for a visa, but had been told "Your presence in this country is undesirable."

Jordan and his lieutenants are now out of jail, and no doubt the scattered handful of Nazis in a few countries who comprise the WUNS will make further efforts to get together.

But their chances of welding a movement in the ideological image of Adolf Hitler seem, at present, remote at best—all the more so should the leaders of the WUNS make any effort whatsoever to enforce Article 10 of the Cotswold Agreements. That section bars membership in the WUNS to national organizations composed of "political nomads, trouble-makers, hoodlums, thrill-seekers and cowards of all stripes," and obviously any such purge would wipe out most of the so-called World Union of National Socialists at one fell swoop.

Conclusion

Here then is the measure of George Rockwell and his American Nazi Party:

To repeat, neither the Commander nor his small, taterdemalion group is of any consequence on the American scene, except as a nuisance. In more than eight years, Rockwell has not succeeded in organizing anything that resembles a movement. His hard core of two or three dozen includes mostly "political nomads, trouble-makers, hoodlums, thrill-seekers, and cowards of all stripes"—to use the words of the Cotswold Agreements. He has perhaps a few hundred sympathizers or supporters scattered around the country.

Neither he nor his organization has any future in the United States. Almost every American detests him, his troopers, and his swastika emblem.

Nevertheless, Rockwell and his ragamuffin band will probably continue to drill in their Arlington backyard—if they can meet the phone bill—and will continue to seek opportunities to bring notoriety to themselves in the press, and on radio and television, as situations arise into which they can inject their outrageous shenanigans.

The resulting coverage they will receive in the mass media, anxious to frustrate their growth by exposing their vile Nazism, will probably continue to give Rockwell and his followers an appearance of substance which the facts belie. . . .(13)

BLACK MUSLIMS
CASE HISTORY OF NEGRO HATE

Increasing protests and demonstrations for Negro equality have projected into the limelight a fanatical black-supremacy group, the Temple of Islam. Better known as the Black Muslims, this pseudo-religious cult has for more than 30 years preached hatred of the white "devil" and advocated total separation of the races. Until a TV exposé four years ago, the Black Muslims were scarcely known to the general public. Since then the movement has grown apace, both in numbers and notoriety.

Although roundly condemned by most Negro leaders, Temple of Islam has been given an inordinate amount of publicity in recent months. The mass media, by virtually giving "equal time" to Black Muslimism, have tended to equate it with reputable Negro movements such as the National Association for the Advancement of Colored People (NAACP), Southern Christian Leadership Conference (Martin Luther King's movement) and the Congress of Racial Equality (CORE). As a result, the Muslims have gained disproportionate status in the public eye, and their spokesmen—principally Minister Malcolm X—have been enocuraged to air the most extreme racist views against whites in general and Jews in particular.

Whitney M. Young, Jr., executive director of the Urban League, told the Ovearseas Press Club on April 19, 1963 that he and heads of other responsible Negro organizations had refused to appear on public programs with Malcolm X. He deplored the inflation of black nationalists by the "white" mass media, commenting: "You wouldn't invite Senator Javits to debate with Rockwell."

Mr. Young attributed the current "white" preoccupation with black supremacy to a type of "mass masochism," arising from feelings of guilt over injustices to the Negro and a continuing reluctance to effect any changes which would improve his lot: "They are saying, 'I won't change, but cuss me out.'"

Facts about the Black Muslims and their standing in the American Negro community are summarized in the following background report.

Leadership: The Temple of Islam was started in Detroit in 1930 by Wallace D. Fard, or Farrad Muhammad, an Arab silk peddler who disappeared in 1934. Little is known about him. The movement has since been in the hands of Elijah Muhammad, born Elijah Poole in 1897 in Sandersville, Ga. For reasons of health, the ailing leader and "prophet" now spends most of his time in Phoenix, Ariz.

Although five of Elijah Muhammad's sons serve as lesser funtionaries in the organization, the leader's chief aide in governing the Nation of Islam is his son-in-law, Raymond Sharieff, Supreme Captain of the Fruit of Islam, a strong-arm organization of well-disciplined young men. Each Black Muslim mosque has a section of the Fruit of Islam, autonomous, highly secret unit charged with defending members and maintaining security throughout the movement. Unit members frisk all males for weapons as they enter meetings, enforce obedience to cult rules, try members for infractions. The section captains are responsible only to Sharieff at Chicago headquarters.

Malcolm X, the movement's most articulate spokesman, is not a relative of Elijah Muhammad. Although the 28-year-old demagogue serves officially only as minister to New York and Washington, he has been popularly mentioned as heir apparent.*

Strength: Beyond the known fact that there are approximately 100 mosques in cities throughout the country, the actual size of Temple of Islam membership remains a matter of conjecture. Mass rallies draw audiences in the thousands, but only a fraction are active Muslims, observing the obligations of the cult. The estimate reported most often is 100,000 members. Othe. estimates, running considerably lower, try to allow for the difficulty of distinguishing sympathizers from members. Commenting on Temple of Islam during a TV interview on June 9, 1963, NAACP executive director Roy Wilkins pointedly compared its 100,000 black segregationists to the 22 million Negroes in America, virtually all of whom want to *de*-segregate.

Doctrine and Program: Affecting to be an Islamic sect, the Temple of Islam is not recognized by official Islamic bodies. As recently as April 15, 1963, for example, it was denounced by Dr. Said Ramadan, secretary of the World Muslim Congress.

Elijah Muhammad preaches a belief in Allah, portrayed as the "Supreme Black Man among the Blacks." A fundamental tenet of the creed is that the white man, evil personified, is a slave master whose rule will end in 1970. Christianity is attacked as a religious tool for enslavement of the blacks. Muslims advocate total separation from whites to avoid corrupting influences. They look toward the ultimate establishment of an independent Black Nation, made up of several states to be ceded to the Black Muslims by the U.S.A.

In the meantime, adherents are tithed and enjoined to set up their own schools, shops and other enterprises. In Chicago, the University of Islam offers schooling through the first 12 grades. Muslim restaurants operate in several cities. Members must follow strict rules of neatness and clean living. Tobacco, liquor and narcotics are forbidden. Pork is taboo. Women wear official white-sheeted garb, Moroccan style. All members drop their last names "because they are slave names", usually substituting

---

* ED. NOTE: In December, 1963 Malcolm X was suspended by Elijah Muhammad for his tasteless and offensive reaction to President Kennedy's death.

"X". Muslims shun the term "Negro" because it too connotes slavery to them.

To spread their message, the Black Muslims claim to be using 50 radio stations. They also publish and distribute nationwide their own bi-weekly, *Muhammad Speaks*, a 24-page tabloid.

Apostle of Hatred: Malcolm X, an adroit demagogue, has participated in numerous radio and TV panel discussions and has served as the subject of newspaper and magazine interviews.

Born in Omaha in 1925, the son of a Baptist preacher, he relates that the Ku Klux Klan burned down the family home in Nebraska when he was six. They settled next in Lansing, Mich. After the father died, the 11 children were scattered, Malcolm winding up in the care of a white family, who treated him well and sent him to a "white" school where his athletic prowess won him a measure of popularity. In his late teens, Malcolm moved on to Harlem, where he became involved in various underworld operations. At 19, he was convicted of grand larceny in Massachusetts, and served seven years in prison. It was here that he got the "message" of Elijah Muhammad, converted and became the Muslim leader's most devoted apostle. He married an ardent believer and now has three children.

Malcolm X today travels throughout the country, organizing, exhorting, rabble-rousing in halls and on street corners, debating with community leaders and officials—and always available for public interviews. In true demagogic fashion, he is able to adapt his manner and language to any audience.

A boastful passage in an interview in *Playboy* magazine (May 1963) summarizes the 38-year-old Muslim's swift rise:

> . . . In 1946, I was sentenced to 8 to 10 years in Cambridge, Mass., as a common thief who had never passed the eight grade. And the next time I went back to Cambridge was in March 1961, as a guest speaker at the Harvard Law School Forum . . .

No one has sounded more unequivocally the intense hatred of the white man that permeates the Black Muslim movement. According to C. Eric Lincoln, writing in *The New South* (January 1963), Malcolm X addressed the following remarks to a Negro audience in Los Angeles on June 3, 1962, shortly after the plane crash which took the lives of 130 persons, 120 of them prominent Atlantans:

> I would like to announce a very beautiful thing that has happened. . . . I got a wire from God today (laughter). . . . well somebody came and told me that he really had answered our prayers in France. . . . He dropped an airplane out of the sky with over 120 white people

on it. . . . We will continue to pray and we hope that every day another plan falls out of the sky. . . . We call on our God—He gets rid of 120 of them at one whop.

While Black Muslimism is basically anti-white, Jews have been singled out for particular attack.

Denouncing Negro organizations as tools of the whites in the *Playboy* interview, Malcolm X spelled out clearly his feelings about Jews:

> Make a true observation about the Jews, and if it doesn't pat him on the back, then he uses his grip on the mass media to label you an anti-Semite. . . . The Jew is always anxious to **advise** the black man. . . . But the Jew that's advising the Negro joins the NAACP, CORE, The Urban League and others. With money donations the Jew gains control, then he sends the black man doing all this wading-in, boring-in, even burying-in—everything but buying-in. . . . No, when there's something worth owning, the Jews got it. . . .

During a TV interview in June 1963, Malcolm X passionately declared that although Jews teach Negroes not to use violence, Jews do not hesitate to resort to violent methods of self-protection when their own group is attacked. He cited the riot that accompanied a street meeting of James H. Madole's neo-Nazi National Renaissance Party in New York on May 25.

As far back as February 1962, the Muslims showed a curious receptivity to the views of fanatic white racists who share their belief in segregation. At the 1962 annual Muslim convention in Chicago, American Nazi Party leader George Lincoln Rockwell told the Muslims: "Elijah Muhammad is the Adolf Hitler of the black man. . . . Elijah Muhammad is a leader who is trying to do what I am trying to do." Ten uniformed ANP storm troopers in the audience delivered the traditional "Heil." Joseph Beauharnais, leader of Chicago's racist White Circle League, also spoke at the convention. The April 1962 issue of *Muhammad Speaks* carried this comment:

> Mr. Rockwell (The American Nazi Party) has spoken well. . . . He endorsed the stand for self that you and I are taking. Why should not you applaud?

Violence: Over the past few years, a number of outbreaks involving Black Muslims have occurred. For example:

In Los Angeles (Apr. 27, 1962), a riot involving police and a score of Black Muslims broke out near the Temple of Islam mosque; one Muslim was fatally shot. In June 1963, most of the 14 cult members arrested were convicted on charges of incitement to riot and assualt.

In Rochester, N.Y. (Jan. 9, 1963), a team of law-enforcement officers accompanied by a police dog entered a building where a Black Muslim meeting was in progress—to investigate a complaint about an armed man on an upper floor. A riot ensued, and the police were badly beaten up. One officer testified a Muslim leader told him no one could enter their meeting hall—"even if there's been a murder there." Fifteen Black Muslims, charged with assualt and inciting to riot, are up for re-trial this fall, after two mistrials.

In Harlem (May 14, 1963), six men severely beat up CBS newsman Ben Holman, a Negro, who was covering a street rally attracting 3,000. Identifying his assailants as Black Muslims, Holman reported they had told him the thrashing was for his recent series on Black Muslimism in the *Chicago Daily News*.

In several parts of the country, jail riots have been attributed to Black Muslim inmates.

Negro Reactions: When Federal Judge Thurgood Marshall was still serving as chief counsel to the NAACP, he declared that Temple of Islam was "run by a bunch of thugs organized from prisons and jails and financed, I am sure, by . . . some Arab group." He further commented that the cult represented a threat to law and order. These remarks were made October 21, 1959, during an address delivered at Princeton University.

Many other eminent American Negroes have denounced black nationalism in no uncertain terms, among them Jackie Robinson, the Rev. Martin Luther King and, as mentioned earlier, Roy Wilkins and Whitney M. Young, Jr. Dr. King, arriving to speak at the Salem Methodist Church in Harlem on June 30, 1963, was the target of eggs hurled by several Negroes; the pastor, Joshua O. Williams, declared that "the only people to fight Dr. King here would be Black Muslims or African Nationalists."

Possibly the most succinct comment on Temple of Islam was written four years ago in the *Daily Defender*, a Negro newspaper published in Chicago, headquarters of the Black Muslim movement:

> How . . . can we promote a cult which duplicates in reverse the animus, the ill will, the hostility of those racial groupings that we decry? The call for a militant "black supremacy," when we are pleading for equality of opportunity, for equal protection under the law, is an arrant invitation to suicide. (14)

THE QUARANTINE TREATMENT

Each of our studies—the Swastika daubings and the case histories of professional bigots—have this in common: publicity, albeit unfavorable, is the breeding ground for increased activity. Counteraction to agitation is so crucial in controlling the spread of hate that it is useful to explore the specifics of the "quarantine treatment" technique. The technique, originally developed by Dr. S. Andhil Fineberg, and refined by him through the years, was given a recent exposition in the January 1960 issue of the Journal of Intergroup Relations. Dr. Fineberg is the Community Relations Consultant of the American Jewish Committee.

That a vendor of bigotry can be stopped only by publicizing him and all his shabby wares is a common but fallacious belief. Failure to denounce him far and wide does not prove he is being ignored. There are successful ways to defeat him, but they are generally indirect.

Consider the bigot's stock in trade—hate literature. It is a hodge-podge of confusing inconsistencies which an astute, open-minded person readily analyzes and rejects. Its pervading trickery is the use of generalizations to make all members of a group appear identical. By constant repetition, it is possible to tag a racial or religious group with one or another reprehensible trait. Sooner or later, those whose vision has been thus distorted will think in stereotypes instead of judging each man on the basis of his own conduct. Thus, even though a man be penniless, he is presumed to share unlimited resources because his group allegedly "controls all the wealth."

To debate the merits of the bigot's statements only strengthens his hand. It is not wise, for example, to assert that Negroes are good neighbors, because he calls them bad neighbors. There are good and bad neighbors in all groups. Any tendency to lump together the members of any group in such characterizations destroys logical thinking about individual merits and rights. Exposing the fallacious reasoning, rather than refuting each specious argument, is the way to lessen the bigot's following.

The extent to which refutation can prove self-defeating was demonstrated during Hitler's rise to power. German Jews and their Christian friends published many books and pamphlets which were described as "anti-anti-Semitic." This tactic only encouraged the Nazis to invent more calumnies.

Experience and research lead to the conclusion that the only good defense is to immunize the public against the bigot's wiles. This requires year-round activity. No one who contributes to such a program of public education can be rightfully accused of "ignoring" any bigot. It is far better to drain the swamps where mosquitoes breed than to try to swat every mosquito.

Normally, when a professional bigot tries to widen his audience through radio, television or reputable newspapers and magazines, he does not succeed. Those who manage the media usually regard with contempt a personality whose only claim to public attention is the ability to provoke controversy by assailing racial and religious groups. There is little willingness to make a professional bigot newsworthy by building his image in the public mind, even as a distateful one. At times, however, bigotry itself is in the news; then the temptation to parade the bigots becomes great.

This occurred after the bombing of the temple in Atlanta, Georgia, in October 1958. Coming, as it did, after seven other bombings and attempted bombings of Jewish institutions within 18 months, coupled with threats of other assaults, the Atlanta incident brought anti-Semitism sharply into public focus. Consequently, there was a sudden splurge of publicity for some previously obscure hatemongers.

One large newspaper chain published a series of five articles about publishers of anti-Semitic literature, with quotes of some of their writings. Among them was George Lincoln Rockwell, previously unknown to the general public, who printed rabid pamphlets in the basement of his home in Arlington, Virginia. After the local newspaper ran his picture and photos of his pamphlets, together with much unfavorable information about him, Rockwell came to the publisher, asking for more. A grand jury charged him with maintaining a public nuisance. Shortly thereafter the police seized some of his propaganda materials. Later, on court order, these were returned. Rockwell used this seizure as an occasion to announce his candidacy for the Virginia State Senate.

Another agitator "exposed" in the series of five articles was Conde McGinley, a notorious publisher of hate literature since 1950. He too prefers obloquy to obscurity. McGinley has been scathingly censured in New Jersey newspapers. Nevertheless, he has obtained adequate financial aid to continue his nefarious business, while many agitators who received no such treatment have petered out. After each public "exposure" it was apparent that he received augmented support; those sharing McGinley's aberrant views were impressed by the evidence that he was making himself known.

A fact too often ignored by those who favor indiscriminate exposure of the professional bigot is that the very act of exposing his calumnies often gives them further circulation. If a man is mentioned in the mass media, not for conduct but for written or spoken words, the words become an essential part of the picture.

When a TV interviewer in the summer of 1959 presented a series of five programs on hate movements in New York's Harlem, the scurrilities which had reached only a few thousand were conveyed to millions of television viewers. Leaders of the hate organizations used the broadcasts as proof that they were becoming highly influential. Members of defamed groups, sitting in their own homes, heard themselve maligned and knew that these canards were likewise reaching their neighbors. When such material is circulated, it reaches people susceptible to bigotry who, far from being repelled, discover to whom they may turn for more servings of intolerance.

The mass media are powerful instruments for promoting good will between groups, for making bigotry unpopular and for fostering a climate of opinion wherein intolerance cannot flourish. Their potency, however, rests upon their own freedom to decide what is newsworthy, and their independence from censorship.

How the media can frustrate individual bigots is a difficult problem, especially when by deliberate trickery these publicity seekers make themselves newsworthy. One of their latest devices is to take advantage of radio programs which broadcast voices coming over the telephone. In Missouri, in the summer of 1959, this method was used to quote a professional hatemonger, give his address and encourage people to subscribe to his periodical. Finally, the popular radio commentator realized that his program was being exploited and was doing more harm than good. Thereafter, he cut off the conversation as soon as a bigoted statement was injected.

That dealing with rabble-rousers calls for restraint became dramatically evident between 1940 and 1946. Several demagogues had gained national notoriety as virulent anti-Semites. When one of them came to St. Louis, Minneapolis, Los Angeles, Detroit, Boston or elsewhere, newspapers would announce his arrival. Thereupon some of the outraged local citizens would picket the meeting hall and demonstrate outside the door. This led in some instances to violent encounters and arrests. If undisturbed, the meetings would not have been considered newsworthy by the local press. But outbreaks and arrests are news indeed.

In September 1946, *Commentary* published an article, "Checkmate for Rabble-Rousers," in which this writer appealed for what he at first called "the silent treatment" of hatemongers. But this technique involved much more than simply remaining silent; therefore in subsequent articles and books, it was termed "the quarantine treatment." For several years, records were kept of what occurred before and after the quarantine treatment was used. In every city the experience was similar to Cleveland's — as described in October 1949 in an editorial of *The Cleveland Plain Dealer:*

When Gerald "the contemptible" Smith first visited Cleveland to pour out his "America First" pusillanimity, a lot of people got worked up, said he ought to be denied a place to speak, and threatened to make trouble. Gerald L. K. Smith thrived on that, for it brought him notoriety, crowds and a full collection plate.

Then we learned how to handle the likes of Gerald L. K. Smith, the rabble-rousers, the dissension breeders of the right and of the left. In this city of proud liberal heritage, we permitted them the freedom of speech guaranteed by the government they revile; but we decided that there was nothing in the Constitution compelling us to listen to them and to pay one damned bit of attention to them.

The result was that Gerald L. K. Smith couldn't attract a corporal's guard to his klan-like orations, and the collection plate didn't hold enough to pay expenses. Gerald "the contemptible" stopped coming.

The American Jewish Committee and other community relations organizations have wholeheartedly supported the quarantine treatment because it provides a means of counteracting bigots without giving them unwarranted publicity or interfering with their freedom of speech.

Whenever the basic rules of free speech are violated, quarantine of hatemongering is impossible. Freedom of speech does not require giving free newspaper space or television time to a public nuisance. But if he gets his own soapbox, he is entitled to its use. Some cry out indignantly that they will not permit public property maintained by their taxes—such as a town hall or school building — to be used by a hate-monger. Yet it is far better that he address a handful of ne'er-do-wells in a public hall than be driven out to greet a sensation-seeking crowd at a nearby meeting place. If handed the martyr's role, the bigot becomes a genuine menace.

Every hatemonger alleges that attempts are being made to deny him freedom of speech. When such a denial actually occurs, it brings to the bigot's support many conscientious citizens who detest his views—genuine liberals to whom freedom of speech is inviolate. The concept of free speech has no meaning if we tolerate only that which we admire.

Suing a bigot for libel renders the quarantine method ineffective. No professional hatemonger has even been put out of business by losing a libel action. Publicity and "martyrdom" have always richly compensated for whatever financial loss he suffered. As reported by this author in an article in 1943, "Can Anti-Semitism Be Outlawed?" the Jews of Germany won over 200 libel suits against anti-Semitic defamers, prior to 1932, and were the worse off for these Pyrrhic victories.

Those who surreptitiously give funds or other assistance to promoters of racial and religious intolerance pose a separate problem. Telling the public about concealed supporters brings the bigot to the fore. But it is often possible to influence anonymous benefactors by giving the facts to their friends—a tedious but rewarding process.

Applying quarantine to vendors of group hatred requires self-restraint, patience and discretion. One must never forget that the ultimate decision whether or not to publicize a professional agitator rests with the publisher, editor, station manager or whoever in each instance decides what the particular medium of communication should transmit. It is altogether proper to provide information concerning obnoxious persons to those who have channels to the public. But furnishing information and explaining the harmful results of advertising the troublemaker are the only permissible steps in dealing with the press, radio and television. Any approach which an editor or broadcaster could regard as an attempt at censorship will inevitably boomerang.

In addition to these principles, several rules of thumb have come from practical experience:

1. Competent community relations organizations should observe the activities of hatemongers and be prepared to furnish adequate information to friendly inquirers.

2. Those who know a rabble-rouser is coming and wish to make his visit ineffective should *privately* expose to opinion molders his character and the kind of message he brings. This includes city officials and heads of organizations who might be persuaded by his misrepresentations to cooperate with him.

3. After a rabble-rouser has rented a hall there should be no public argument about it. If the proprietor of the hall has an indisputable right to cancel, he is justified in doing so. But if cancelling provides a legitimate grievance for the hatemonger, he should not be asked to withdraw.

4. If a bigot or his literature is being promoted in the community, the situation should be used constructively—to induce more people to interest themselves in projects for improving intergroup relations.

During the past 20 years, greater effort has been made in the United States to determine the causes of group prejudice and to find means to counteract this social malady than in all of previous history. Nowhere else has there been a comparable endeavor to deal with this problem on a scientific basis. Today we restrain the impulse to counter malicious provocation with logical answers and to exaggerate the power of each bothersome bigot. Today we are less concerned with what each rabble-rouser says or even does, provided he does not ask his hearers to commit acts of violence. We know we must rather give attention to the public's attitudes and the need for democratic relations among members of all groups. From the task of helping strengthen the American way of life, no promoter of bigotry should divert us. The social disease he seeks to spread is best treated by quarantine.(15)

THE "LOVE" ETHIC

In contemporary America, it has been the issue of desegregation which has triggered the hate mechanism and set in motion the dynamics of prejudice—the latent insecurities of people who feel threatened, the agitators who dramatize these insecurities, the violence that is the product of mob rule motivated by hate. But it has had its counterpoint—in the restraint, the dignity of the victims—and in the action concept of non-violence. Its most articulate exponent—in all probability, its conceiver—has been the Reverend Martin Luther King, who gives to the terms "non-violence" and "love," not the softness of capitulation, but the firmness and understanding of being right.

The following excerpts are from his interview with Dr. Kenneth B. Clark, which Dr. Clark subsequently edited for publication in *The Negro Protest*.

. . . Non-violent direct action is a method of acting to rectify a social situation that is unjust and it involves engaging in a practical technique that nullifies the use of violence and calls for non-violence at every point. That is, you don't use physical violence against the opponent. Now, the love ethic is another dimension which goes into the realm of accepting non-violence as a way of life. There are many people who will accept non-violence as the most practical technique to be used in a social situation, but they would not go to the point of seeing the necessity of accepting non-violence as a way of life. Now, I accept both. I think that non-violent resistance is the most potent weapon available to oppressed people in their struggle for freedom and human dignity. It has a way of disarming the opponent. It exposes his moral defenses. It weakens his morale and at the same time it works on his conscience. He just doesn't know how to handle it and I have seen this over and over again in our struggle in the South. . . .

. . . I think one has to understand the meaning of "love" at this point. I'm certainly not thinking of an affectionate response.

I think it is really nonsense to urge oppressed peoples to love their oppressors in an affectionate sense. . . . I don't think of love, as in this context, as emotional bosh. I don't think of it as a weak force, but I think of love as something strong and that organizes itself into powerful direct action. Now this is what I try to teach in this struggle in the South: that we are not engaged in a struggle that means we sit down and do nothing; that there is a great deal of difference between non-resistance to evil and non-violent resistance. Non-resistance leaves you in a state of stagnant passivity and deadly complacency where non-violent resistance means that you do resist in a very strong and determined manner and I think some of the criticism of non-violence or some of the critics fail to realize that we are talking about something very strong and they confuse non-resistance with non-violent resistance. . . . If anyone has ever lived with a non-violent movement in the South, from Montgomery on through the freedom rides and through the sit-in movement and the recent Birmingham movement and seen the reactions of many of the extremists and reactionaries in the white community, he wouldn't say that this movement makes—this philosophy makes them comfortable. I think it arouses a sense of shame within them often—in many instances. I think it does something to touch the conscience and establish a sense of guilt. Now so often people respond to guilt by engaging more in the guilt-evoking act in an attempt to drown the sense of guilt, but this approach certainly doesn't make the white man feel comfortable. I think it does the other thing. It disturbs his conscience and it disturbs this sense of contentment that he's had. . . .

. . . these brutal methods used by the Birmingham police force and other police forces will naturally arouse the ire of Negroes and I think there is the danger that some will be so aroused that they will retaliate with violence. I think though that we can be sure that the vast majority of Negroes who engage in the demonstrations and who understand the non-violent philosophy will be able to face dogs and all of the other brutal methods that are used without retaliating with violence because they understand that one of the first principles of non-violence is the willingness to be the recipient of violence while never inflicting violence upon another. . . . I think there is a contagious quality in a movement like this when everybody talks about non-violence and being faithful to it and being dignified in your resistance. It tends to get over to the larger group because this becomes a part of the vocabulary of the movement.(16)

Amid the violence and hate, it is the young who suffer the most. Often, they are even too young to understand the role in which they have been cast. Who can forget the frightened little Negro children being shepherded among hostile, jeering crowds to a newly integrated public school somewhere in the Deep South? A sensitive analysis of the Negro child, "The Negro Child Asks: Why?" by Margaret Anderson, a Tennessee public school teacher and guidance director, appeared in the New York Times Magazine, December 1, 1963.

Today, as the Negro in America struggles to gain his constitutional rights, his children bear the imprint of his ordeal. The impressions created in their minds during these days of social upheaval will affect the future of race relations in this country. As I have looked into their eyes and talked with them—across a desk, on a dusty playground, or in a mountain cabin with newspaper-covered walls—I have thought how carefully we would set examples and teach them, *if* we were wise.

Otherwise, as one white man said: "We may see the day when we will wish for men like Martin Luther King, and regret the time that Congress procrastinated for political expediencies."

Nowhere is the turbulence which accompanies the Negro's drive for freedom more evident than in desegregated classrooms. There, Negro children show an extreme dedication to the social revolution about them. They are informed on racial problems throughout the nation and sensitive to events of the day in so far as their cause could be affected by them.

The saddest of these was Nov. 22 when, during afternoon classes, the news came that President Kennedy had been wounded.

"Oh, no," whispered a young Negro girl in a history class where the group was studying the process of democratic government. She buried her head on her desk.

Then, with the white students, the Negro students waited in shock and dismay, unwilling to accept reality—each hoping and praying to himself that the President still breathed.

With the final announcement, a Negro girl said, "He was our friend. Lord knows he was our friend. What will happen to us now?"

For Negro children there have been other sad days—of different magnitude, but days that left indelible impressions.

Robyn, a Negro student now in college, spoke of the murder of the four Negro girls in the Birmingham church: "I was sick that day. I was angry, too. I didn't know at whom I was angry, but I felt as if someone had done something directly to me— not to my race, but to me as an individual."

Another spoke of the same incident. "It hurts," he said. "Any one of those girls could have been my sister. Don't you think I don't know that?"

Marie does know. Now in high school, she was 9 years old when dynamite was thrown into her house in the late hours of the night. Her family had to move to another community for shelter.

"I was asleep when it happened," she said. "It pretty well wrecked our house. I rushed out of bed and ran to my mother. There were cars outside all up and down the road. People were excited. I looked out. There were only strange faces. All I could think was: 'Why would they do this to us?'

"You see, my mother had always told us that white people were friendly. She said that if we got sick, or ran out of food, white people would help us. I couldn't understand. If they were like she said, then why would they want to kill us? Why?

"For a long time then I hated white people.

"Sometimes, when the teacher asks who knows the answer to a question, and a white student raises his hand first, I'm afraid to raise my hand. I know the answer, but something keeps me from raising my hand. I think back to: 'Why?' It's always: 'Why?'

"I think about those horrible things that occur every day. I'm trying to learn to rationalize and not feel hatred. Every night, I spend a few minutes trying to figure things out. Sometimes I think I have a half-way answer. I'm beginning to understand more now about the reasons the white people feel the way they do. They can't change overnight any more than we can. We've all got to understand each other and change together."

She relaxed somewhat and looked far away. "But then, she said, "there's always that Why?"

Another Negro girl said, "I don't worry about myself any more, but I do worry about my relatives in Alabama. I always think: "What if it had been my father they dragged down the street?"

"Well, I didn't think of this as a racial problem," said a Negro boy, "I just thought how horrible it was that one human being would want to kill another—and in a church."

Although the Negro child does not readily admit he is afraid for himself alone, there is a mental anguish generated by the turmoil and dissention about him which is confusing.

"I think," said a Negro teacher who works in a segregated school, "that my students were more disturbed by events in Americus, Ga., where people were jailed under an archaic law. . . . We had just concluded a study of the Constitution when this happened. They couldn't reconcile what they had learned in school with this action.

"Whenever trouble occurs, the children are restless. They seem to feel they should be helping. Sometimes, they make up petitions to send to officials. Many write letters. Some take part in the demonstration wherever possible. This partly satisfies their desire to help."

But then, no matter to what Negro child one talks, fear is ever present. It is a kind of instinctive fear that is engrained in servitude. It culminates in humility and the crushing of the human spirit. It is revealed in such questions as:

"Will I be able to play ball with the white boys?"

"Will there be a place for me when the class goes on an overnight field trip? Where will I eat and sleep?

"Will there be someone who will walk down the aisle with me on graduation night?

It is the kind of fear that makes a child wonder who he is— and why. It is an awful fear to witness in American children. Yet, they appear to grapple with it as a part of their daily lives, really expecting to face little else.

Listen again to Robyn. An elderly teacher once said of him, "He has the most brilliant mind of any student I have ever taught." To recount his experiences from the time he came to us from a small country school so remote from the main stream of America that I wondered how he could have accumulated such knowledge, and on to his graduation among the top in his class, would be a story in itself. Let it stand here to say he is making a brilliant record in college.

"Do I feel like giving up?" he asked.

"No," he said, "because the struggle has just begun to reach a place of culmination. These incidents give me a better look at the situation and what I must face. . . . Since others have died, I am more urged to go on and do my part. It's like the Rev. Dr. King said: 'A goal that is not worth dying for is not worth having.'

"I'll face many problems. I see now that I must meet, face, interpret and use them to make my life an example of what my race can do and be."

As the young Negro strives to uplift himself amid the uncertainties of the day, there are pronounced inner drives which, I feel, are honorable forces in this great human struggle. Anyone who has worked closely with Negro children can see that these forces are present and must be reckoned with.

First, the young Negro today is deliberately and immediately dedicated to planned change. He might be described as one in a state of marginality. He is striving to pull himself out of the old culture and into a new culture, somewhat as the children of immigrants must strive to learn to move freely in a new society.

The remarkable fact is that by simple determination he appears to be coming through his marginal state faster than dreamed of, perhaps by himself or by us a few years ago. Certainly, he is dispelling many of the claims of white supremacists.

Becky, I thought, explained this determination to change quite plainly. She was asked to play the part of a Negro servant of the old days in a high school play. The teacher had hoped to befriend her, and envisioned her participation as an opportunity for her.

"This part," the teacher said, "was made for you."

Becky examined the script, which was written in the dialect of the days before the Civil War. There were words like "mawnin'" for "morning,' "gwine" for "going," "dis" for "this" and "bees" for "is." The child returned the script to her teacher and said: "No, ma'm, we don't talk like that no more."

The teacher tried again, for the part was really that of the heroine. "You see, Becky, the part was made for you," she said. "You are the only one who can really do it. Everyone will love you for it."

The thinking young girl looked back at her teacher and insisted respectfully: "No, ma'm. We don't talk like that no more." No amount of persuasion on the part of the teacher or Becky's classmates could change her mind. It was as if she had left home to seek her fortune; and never, never again would she return to the age of the rural "folk Negro."

Secondly, the young Negro is beginning to see the importance of self-development and the acceptance of responsibility. He is trying desperately to improve himself, against tremendous social, political and economic obstacles. Marie expressed it this way:

"This drive to move ahead and make somthing of ourselves is a powerful force. We know that in anything we do, we have got to be the best."

She went on: "You know, my grandmother never learned to read, but she could count a little. My mother only got to the fourth grade. When I started studying algebra, she tried to study with me: I saw she could have learned it if she had had a chance.

"My father never got to high school, but he has a brilliant mind in mechanics. I know that now. My grandmother says I'm the first of her grandchilden to come through high school. You see how important this is to me?"

"Your grandmother must be very proud of you," I said, for Marie is an honor student.

"Yes," she answered. "She's proud and I want her to live to see me do something. . . . There are many forces that drive us, but this is one of the most powerful."

That moment, I was proud and sad for Marie all at the same time. Obviously, such children are under a tremendous pressure to achieve. As she says: "All about us, people are saying, 'Do this—do that—if you want to be a first-class citizen.'"

I wondered if this generation of Negro children would ever really know real peace of mind. Of would they all their lives be occupied with claiming their rights as human beings? To one way of thinking, such children are prisoners to problems we have not solved. But from what I have seen thus far, I do believe they will unleash themselves.

So, while Marie wipes the perspiration from her hands and relates the importance of self-development, another expresses eagerness to accept the responsibility for himself.

James is a tall, clean, 10th grade boy with a contagious smile. On one of his happy days, he rushed up to my office with another Negro boy. The two stood in the doorway. In our conversation about the headlines of the day, James said: "We're coming—slowly but surely we're coming." His eyes sparkled.

"Perhaps not as slowly as you may think," I answered, thinking back to the time, seeming only yesterday, when I had seen his brothers come to the white school as frightened children who cowered against the walls in the corridors and were so tense they were barely able to speak. Now, in a comparatively safe atmosphere, it is a wonderful privilege to see the real children who were there all the time with dormant talents waiting for expression.

"Well, yes," he smiled. "I'm looking forward to moving on now and being ready. We'll be ready. You'll see," he said, as if he were making a promise and the millennium would be tomorrow. The younger boy with him smiled approval.

When they had gone, I though to myself, "God, preserve the spirit of these children to all eternity." You see, when an individual accepts the responsibility for his own success or failure, he has already made tremendous progress.

Never before has the young Negro been so eager to work and learn. Never before has he liked himself so much—and he has had to learn to like himself. He has come far enough in the past decade to realize initial accomplishment in many fields. He now has examples in his own race to look to. He exhibits pride in the success of his contemporaries. It is the sort of pride

I can imagine the early pioneers must have felt when they crossed a mountain, or cut down a forest.

It would seem that in this atmosphere, when the young Negro is intent on self-improvement, it would be wise to help him. There is so much to be accomplished by all of our children, and the days of youth are fleeting.

Practically eveery Negro student with whom I have talked at some time speaks of helping others. He feels a deep obligation to his people.

Robyn had said before he left for college this fall: "I know I've got to prepare myself. We talked on of his interest in science and research, and of how, perhaps, after college he would attend a university where he would do graduate study. Then he said: "There's another way I've got to be trained— maybe in social work—in order to be ready to help. It is the duty of everyone. Anyone who has bettered himself in any way should strive to bring up the rest of us. I have got to be ready to help and to give something."

He mentioned his own poverty lightly. "There are those so much poorer," he said.

This feeling of dedication carries over to the way the older Negro students look after the younger ones, even in the daily routine of school work. For example, on one occasion, some Negro children who came to register for school did not know their birth dates. One of the older boys stepped forward and gave the information. He had memorized it, knowing it would be needed.

Is it not an honorable quality that the strong should show concern for those less fortunate in whatever way? History has shown time and time again that when a group of people pull together for the welfare of all they gather together a tremendous strength, and the young Negro today exhibits courage. He has not only the kind of courage that has provided him the strength to endure every known effrontery to human dignity, but the kind of courage Becky showed when she said to her teacher, "No, ma'm we don't talk like that no more."

"And courage," said Sir Winston Churchill, "is the first of human qualities, for it is the quality which guarantees all others."

It would seem that a great hope lies in acknowledging the good that is present in these powerful human forces. Certainly, we have seen there is little to be gained by perpetuating injustice. True, I have looked for the good. It is there. It is in children everywhere. And as the Negro youth rises to forge his dreams and the dreams of his forebears, to which he is still prisoner, it would be my hope that we would rise with him to ease these human conditions, and bring stature to our national character.(17)

Perhaps the most eloquent statement of the overriding American need and responsibility to end the internecine strife of Negro and white comes from the pen of James Baldwin, outstanding Negro author and novelist. In *The Fire Next Time,* he talks to the entire country in a way that must necessarily come as a rude shock to the smug and the complacent.

White Americans find it as difficult as white people elsewhere to divest themselves of the notion that they are in possession of some intrinsic value that black people need, or want. And this assumption—which, for example, makes the solution to the Negro problem depend on the speed with which Negroes accept and adopt white standards—is revealed in all kinds of striking ways, from Bobby Kennedy's assurance that a Negro can become President in forty years to the unfortunate tone of warm congratulation with which so many liberals address their Negro equals. It is the Negro, of course, who is presumed to have become equal—an achievement that not only proves the comforting fact that perseverance has no color, but also overwhelmingly corroborates the white man's sense of his own value.

Alas, this value can scarcely be corroborated in any other way; there is certainly little enough in the white man's public or private life that one should desire to imitate. . . . How can one respect, let alone adopt, the values of a people who do not, on any level whatever, live the way they say they do, or the way they say they should? . . . White people cannot, in the generality, be taken as models of how to live.Rather, the white man is himself in sore need of new standards, which will release him from his confusion and place him once again in fruitful communion with the depths of his own being. . . .

In short, we, the black and white, deeply need each other here if we are really to become a nation—if we are really, that is, to achieve our identity, our maturity, as men and women. To create one nation has proved to be a hideously difficult task; there is certainly no need now to create two, one black and one white. But white men with far more political power than that possessed by the Nation of Islam movement (Black Muslims) have been advocating exactly this, in effect, for generations. If this sentiment is honored when it falls from the lips of Senator Byrd, then there is no reason it should not be honored when it falls from the lips of Malcolm X. And any Congressional committee wishing to investigate the latter must also be willing to investigate the former. They are expressing exactly the same sentiments and represent exactly the same danger. . . .

The American Negro has the great advantage of having never believed that collection of myths to which white Americans cling: that their ancestors were all freedom-loving heroes, that they were born in the greatest country the world has even seen, or that Americans are invincible in battle and wise in peace, that Americans have always dealt honorably with Mexicans and Indians and all other neighbors or inferiors, that American men are the world's most direct and virile, that American women are pure. Negroes know far more about white Americans that that; it can almost be said, in fact, they they know about white Americans what parents—or, anyway, mothers— know about their children, and that they very often regard white Americans that way. . . . (Ask any Negro what he knows about white people with whom he works. And then ask the white people with whom he works what they know about *him*).(18)

Intertwined with this plausibly bitter appraisal of the white American is a passage that is of the essence of understanding the Negro—his past struggles and his present and future goals.

This past, the Negro's past, of robe, fire, torture, castration, infanticide, rape; death and humiliation; fear by day and night, fear as deep as the marrow of the bone; doubt that he was worthy of life, since everyone around him denied it; sorrow for women, for his kinfolk, for his children, who needed his protection, and whom he could not protect; rage, hatered, and murder, hatred for white men so deep that it often turned against him and his own, and made all love, all trust, all joy impossible—this past, this endless struggle to achieve and reveal and confirm a human identity, human authority, yet contains, for all its horror, something very beautiful.

I do not mean to be sentimental about suffering—enough is certainly as good as a feast—but people who cannot suffer can never grow up, can never discover who they are. That man who is forced each day to snatch his manhood, his identity, out of the fire of human cruelty that rages to destroy it knows, if he survives his effort, and even if he does not survive it, something about himself and human life that no school on earth— and, indeed, no church—can teach. He achieves his own authority, and that is unshakable. This is because, in order to save his life, he is forced to look beneath appearances, to take nothing for granted, to hear the meaning behind the words. If one is continually surviving the worst that life can bring, one eventually ceases to be controlled by a fear of what life can bring, whatever it brings must be borne. And at this level of experience one's bitterness begins to be palatable, and hatred becomes too heavy a sack to carry. The apprehension of life here so briefly and inadequately sketched has been the experience of generations of Negroes, and it helps to explain how they have endured and how they have been able to produce children of kindergarten age who can walk through mobs to get to school.

It demands great force and great cunning continually to assault the mighty and indifferent fortress of white supremacy, as Negroes in this country have done so long. It demands great spiritual resilience not to hate the hater whose foot is on your neck, and an even greater miracle of perception and charity not to teach your child to hate. The Negro boys and girls who are facing mobs today come out of a long line of improbable aristocrats—the only genuine aristocrats this country has produced. I say "this country" because their frame of reference was totally American. They were hewing out of the mountain of white supremacy the stone of their individuality..

I have great respect for that unsung army of black men and women who trudged down back lanes and entered back doors saying "Yes, sir" and "No, Ma'am" in order to acquire a new roof for the schoolhouse, new books, a new chemistry lab, more beds for the domitories, more dormitories. They did not like saying "Yes, sir" and "No, Ma'am," but the country was in no hurry to educate Negroes, these black men and women knew that the job had to be done and they put their pride in their pockets in order to do it.

It is very hard to believe that they were in any way inferior to the white men and women who opened those back doors. It is very hard to believe that those men and women, raising their children, eating their greens, crying their curses, weeping their tears, singing their songs, making their love, as the sun rose, as the sun set, were in any way inferior to the white men and women who crept over to share these splendors after the sun went down. . . . I am proud of these people not because of their color but because of their intelligence and their spiritual force and their beauty. The country should be proud of them, too, but alas, not many people in this country even know of their existence. And the reason for this ignorance is that a knowledge of the role these people played—and play—in American life would reveal more about America to Americans than Americans wish to know. . . .(19)

SECTION III

THE POLITICS OF HATE

THE POLITICS OF HATE

The Radical Right is the name currently being applied to the extreme right-wing segment of American life, a movement which embraces "hate" as a major tenet of its program. The name emerges from a concept that the extreme right-wing of political thought and action in this country is not really conservative, as it pretends, but rather is revolutionary in character. Historians of the contemporary American scene point out that while the leaders of this movement seem to exalt the "traditional" values in American life, in actuality they are opposed to democratic principles and would subvert them in the name of fighting communism. This section will seek to explore 1) the background and history of the Radical Right in contemporary American society; 2) the sources of the strength and following of the movement; and 3) the direct and subtle ways in which the rationale of hate is employed as a weapon of political action.

THE RADICAL RIGHT
BACKGROUND AND HISTORY

To understand the significance of the Radical Right in America today, the movement must be set against the background of total American society as it continues to emerge to maturity and world responsibility. For implicit in this process is the requirement of flexibility and adjustment in a world which seems ever new and ever threatening.

The normal anxiety of our society is graphically captured by Professor Andrew Hacker in his article, "What Kind of Nation Are We?" carried in the New York Times Magazine of December 8, 1963.

America is a complex of individuals and institutions, each shaping the values and behavior of the other. While only a quarter of a century from our bicentennial, we are still a new nation, pioneering on many frontiers and haunted by a maze of unresolved problems. Perhaps what characterizes America best is the sense of movement, our readiness to embark on new ventures and our willingness to adjust ourselves to major transformations in our national life. A description of the country we are, therefore, cannot help but be, in part, a description of the society we are becoming.

We are, first and foremost, a democracy. Indeed, of all the major countries of the world, we are probably the most democratic in feeling and actions. To be sure, the will of the majority is not reflected in many of our political institutions. In the Congress, in state legislatures and in a thousand city halls and county court-houses, well-entrenched minorities have their way. But this is partly because there is no coherent and continuing majority; and even if there were, it is not clear that this aggregate would have a "will" demanding to be translated into legislation.

Perhaps this is only another way of saying that America is not really a "political" nation. For most of us, affairs of state come well down in our list of personal concerns. Only a few petition, picket or even participate on a sustained basis. Democracy, therefore, must be interpreted as a social rather than a political phenomenon. It has meant that a greater and greater number of Americans have been able to ascend to a level of material security and a consciousness of personal worth that in other countries remain the privilege of exclusive minorities.

It is this democratic psychology that troubles critics of America more than anything else. The typical citizen is seen as overly opinionated and overly concerned with what society owes to him. Thus American entertainment is labeled "mass culture," American education is "life-adjustment," and American politics are a series of "popularity contests." Moreover, Americans are seen as demanding as a right admission to higher education, to executive and professional occupations—in fact, to whatever citadels of privilege and prestige society has to offer. The principle of equality is no longer a textbook rubric but the notion that all opinions and talents are of equal quality.

More serious is the charge that there exists little public enthusiasm for those who defy accepted conventions. Our reluctance to tolerate unpopular ideas is a national characteristic having deep roots. Traditional assumptions about innocence until guilt is proven, about the status of those who refuse to incriminate themselves, about the free market-place of ideas—these defenses of individual freedom find little popular support when put to the acid test. While an American majority may be hard to discover on most issues, there is a consensus here. There is the feeling that ideas can be corrupting and that accused enemies of society should be locked up with a minimum of formality. Most Americans share this tough-minded sentiment, and while sincerely shocked by open violence, they are prepared to assume that liberty is for those who are not suspected of abusing it.

Yet critics of the American temper are, in reality, decrying the fact that social classes play so small a role in our national life. Political democracy has a long history in Western Europe but it has been hedged in by class barriers that kept the bulk of its citizens in what was to be their proper stations. Here and there, the feudal tradition lingers on, and the public remains deferential to its "betters."

Those who emigrated to America broke with this tradition of deference, and in so doing embraced the view that everyone has the right to whatever ambitions he cares to set for himself. The foundation stone of American democracy, then, is its classlessness, its opportunities for mobility for tens of millions rather than for a handful in each generation.

Only in America is it so certain that a majority will go on to college, wear a white collar at work and experience a style of life hitherto reserved for those born to privilege. Without a doubt, Michigan State University will never be an Oxford; the executives of United States Steel will not have the polish of the governors of the Bank of England; and the output of Hollywood will fail to rival the standards of a Fellini or a Bergman.

But style, tone and sensitivity are no more typical of a majority of Europeans than of Americans. The difference is that we refuse to keep down whole classes just because their rise may rend the fabric of culture and civility. America pays a price for its egalitarian principles, but the cost is small compared with the vistas and opportunities that have opened to countless citizens.

And, so long as one is a "good American," vague as that criterion may be, religious and ethnic considerations are viewed as secondary. The melting pot is doing its work—especially on those under the ages of 40—and while its product may be blandly homogeneous, it must not be forgotten that graduation to the status of American is a marked advance for those who have succeeded in this climb.

Sociologists are fond of talking about the alienation and the quest for "identity" that plague the new middle class and even the affluent working class. Yet for most, the relief from crowded slums, desolate small towns and immigrant identities has been a liberating experience. The problem is how to use this freedom, and not to question its existence.

But talk of a homogeneous national character must be tempered by a recognition that there are still several Americas, certainly so far as values and outlook are concerned.

There is, for example, the America of the provinces, belonging to those who remain on farms and in small towns and medium-sized cities. This continues to be conservative country, adhering to the principles of limited government, small business and the ingrown community. Provincial America is well represented in Congress by both political parties and has a major say in the affairs of our Government. This nation within a nation is on the decline in social and economic terms, but its power in legislative councils gives its viewpoint not only a hearing but often a political veto.

Yet alongside it is a growing metropolitan America, typified by the new suburbs more than the cities and by national corporations as much as by the Executive branch of the Federal Government. Tens of millions of Americans have left small towns and the countryside in recent decades, leaving behind their provincial values and adjusting to the unspoken rules of metropolitan life. The suburbs and the corporations, both destined to grow, require a new style—best characterized as moderate, modern and uncontroversial.

There is not a little soul-searching about the new thinking in economics, education and religion that metropolitan life encourages, and there are serious reactions—"return to fundamentals"—from time to time. Many of the tensions of the nation arise because of the conflicts between provincial and metropolitan values. This confrontation is often expressed in our much-publicized quests for "national values" and our yearning to rediscover "democratic principles." Yet when all is said and done, the answer is that such goals and principles will be influenced by our new technology and the ways we organize society to meet the needs of the machines we have created.

For looming over the social scene is technological America, a new association of machines and ideas that staggers the imagination. The nation's economy, again more than that of any other country, has transformed patterns of production and employment beyond recognition.

This is testimony to America's willingness to experiment, to take risks and to adapt itself to new organizational forms and productive processes. Neither automation nor the corporations have social theories to justify their existence; they arise from the drawing boards of engineers and the deliberations of executives. The new economy has no ideology, but millions are taking their places in it and partaking of the incomes and advantages it is able to bestow.

The electronic computer is a monument to America's industrial rationality, to the ability of man to apply his reason to the raw materials of the world around him. The thousands of engineers at I.B.M., at A.T. & T. and at N.A.S.A. are not spectacular men, but they have helped to create and utilize technological knowledge on a spectacular scale.

What is clear is that they nor others have the knowledge or skills to facilitate the adjustment of society to the new machines. A continuing dilemma of history has been the lag between the productive instruments brought into being by human rationality and the failure of that rationality to organize means of coping with the social consequences of industrial progress. Yet another

America, a society of losers, has become the discard heap of the new technology.

The affluence of America is widespread but it is far from universal. Millions have failed to find places for themselves in the new economy. Their problem is more than political. The measures devised by liberals—retraining, fiscal reform, expanded welfare services—will have only a marginal impact on the disruptions we are experiencing.

Those of the conservatives—a freer market mechanism, annual balanced budgets, state rather than Federal action—hold out as little promise. Neither public opinion nor our political institutions can fully understand or devise workable solutions for the plight of those left behind in the wake of the new machines.

Much the same can be said of the overriding domestic issue —civil rights. Insensitivity to the liberties of dissenting or deviating individuals is a small problem compared with the unwillingness to accept Negro Americans as full citizens. The irony, it has often been remarked, is that we have not a "Negro problem" but a problem in the anxieties of white citizens. All that has been said about equality, opportunity and assimilation must be construed as applying to white Americans.

Moreover, the white population is patently unequipped, socially and psychologically, to accept their Negro fellow-citizens as if the color of one's skin made no difference. The reasons why the 90 per cent are so fearful of the 10 per cent are complex, but whether we think of bombings in Birmingham or of flights to the suburbs in the North, the root cause is the same: white Americans, most of them newly arrived in status, sense their vulnerability to those whose proximity might endanger their position in society.

Legislation, if and when passed, may create as many problems as it solves. Backed by the authority of Government, Negroes will have access to places formerly closed to them—access, indeed, to the facilities and opportunities of white America. But white Americans will grow increasingly resentful at such instrusions, and tensions will continue to mount. The problem will have to resolve itself, and the changes that take place will be largely outside the realms of law and politics.

Civil rights has laid bare a nation's weakness. The reluctance of the white majority to make personal sacrifices has been revealed, both to themselves and to the world, and it has shown that the traditional critique of democracy—the tendency of the majority to oppress the minority—has yet to be fully answered.

If America is to be summed up, it is a product of democratic and technological forces each acting and reacting to shape the

other. Our committments to a democratic society and to technological innovation are our most marked characteristics, bringing personal freedom and unequalled prosperity but also producing serious tensions and disruptions in our daily lives.

If the events leading to President Kennedy's death were unpredictable and unpreventable, so are many of the larger developments that give form to our national character and institutions. Much of our time and energy is consumed in adjusting
to the unforeseen consequences of the ideas we embrace with an
enthusiasm that is uniquely American. Our problems are those
of success, and our failures are visible because we are continually conscious of the standards we have set and failed to
meet. (20)

Professor Hacker's succinct recapitulation of today's American society
touches on most of the major sources of the Radical Right which, conceiv-
ably, can be viewed as the intensification of reactions probably held in
free-floating lesser degree by most citizens.

Thus, the person who cannot accept for himself the social mobility of
American life and would prefer to perpetuate the distinctions of caste and
class is likely to be responsive to the Radical Right.

Similarly, the person whose background is "provincial" as distinguished
from "metropolitan;" his oversensitivity will lead him to fight the inevitable
shift of power.

The "fundamentalist," with his insistence on solving today's problems
with yesterday's answers is likewise a Radical Right candidate.

Issues of civil liberties and civil rights, of conformity in thought and
action, of segregation and integration, of how to combat foreign "isms"
provide the basis for polarizing views and establishing a common political
denominator among people who might otherwise have very little in
common.

What is fearsome from the standpoint of the future of our society is that
since the politics of hate represents essentially an extreme polarization process, the healthy political American is distinguishable from the extremist
only as a matter of degree—just as mental health in today's anxious world
is probably only removed by degree from neurosis, psychosis and insanity.
Given the catastrophic event that could trigger an entire nation, who is to
say that the politics of hate—the Radical Right—could not come into the
ascendancy? Is not this something of the process that transformed the
great western civilization that was Germany into the atavistic chauvinism
that was Nazism?

Professor Richard Hofstadter, writing in 1955, utilized essentially psychological processes in defining the *pseudo-conservative,* the prototype of the
Radical Right follower. While, in an article written in 1962, and published
with his first piece in a truly historic document, *The Radical Right,* Professor Hoftsadter somewhat attenuates his earlier views, the psychology of
the pseudo-conservative remains an important ingredient of Radical Right
political philosophy.

Twenty years ago the dynamic force in American political life
came from the side of liberal dissent, from the impulse to reform
the inequities of our economic and social system and to change

our ways of doing things, to the end that the sufferings of the Great Depression would never be repeated. Today the dynamic force in our political life no longer comes from the liberals who made the New Deal possible. By 1952 the liberals had had at least the trappings of power for twenty years. They could look back to a brief, exciting period in the mid-thirties when they had held power itself and had been able to transform the economic and administrative life of the nation. After twenty years the New Deal liberals have quite unconsciously taken on the psychology of those who have entered into possession. Moreover, a large part of the New Deal public, the jobless, distracted and bewildered men of 1933, have in the course of the years substantial places in society for themselves, have become homeowners, suburbanites and solid citizens. Many of them still keep the emotional commitments to the liberal dissent with which they grew up politically, but their social position is one of solid comfort. Among them the dominant tone has become one of satisfaction, even of a kind of conservatism. Insofar as Adlai Stevenson won their enthusiasm in 1952, it was not in spite of, but in part because of the air of poised and reliable conservatism that he brought to the Democratic convention. By comparison, Harry Truman's impassioned rhetoric, with its occasional thrusts at "Wall Street," seemed passé and rather embarrassing. The change did not escape Stevenson himself. "The strange alchemy of time," he said in a speech at Columbus, "has somehow converted the Democrats into the truly conservative party of this country—the party dedicated to conserving all that is best, and building solidly and safely on these foundations." The most that the old liberals can now envisage is not to carry on with some ambitious new program, but simply to defend as much as possible of the old achievements and to try to keep traditional liberties of expression that are threatened.

There is however, a dynamic of dissent in America today. Representing no more than a modest fraction of the electorate, it is not so powerful as the liberal dissent of the New Deal era, but it is powerful enough to set the tone of our political life and to establish throughout the country a kind of punitive reaction. The new dissent is certainly not radical—there are hardly any radicals of any sort left—nor is it precisely conservative. Unlike most of the liberal dissent of the past, the new dissent not only has no respect for non-conformism, but is based upon a relentless demand for conformity. It can most accurately be called pseudo-conservative—I borrow the term from the study of "The Authoritarian Personality" published five years ago by Theodore W. Adorno and his associates—because its exponents, although they believe themselves to be conservatives and usually employ the rhetoric of conservatism, show signs of a serious and restless dissatisfaction with American life, traditions and institutions. They have little in common with the temperate and compromising spirit of true conservatism in the classical sense of the word, and they are far from pleased with the dominant practical conservatism of the moment as it is represented by the Eisenhower administration. Their political reactions express rather a profound if largely unconscious hatred of our society and it ways —a hatred which one would hesitate to impute to them if one did not have suggestive clinical evidence.

From clinical interviews and thematic apperception tests, Adorno and his co-workers found that their pseudo-conservative subjects, although given to a form of political expression that combines a curious mixture of largely conservative with occasional radical notions, succeed in concealing from themselves impulsive tendencies that, if released in action, would be very far from conservative. The pseudo-conservative, Adorno writes, shows "conventionality and authoritarian submissiveness" in his conscious thinking and "violence, anarchic impulses, and chaotic destructiveness in the unconscious sphere. . . . The pseudo conservative is a man who, in the name of upholding traditional American values and institutions and defending them against more or less fictitious dangers, consciously or unconsciously aims at their abolition."

The restlessness, suspicion and fear manifested in various phases of the pseudo-conservative revolt give evidence of the real suffering which the pseudo-conservative experiences in his capacity as a citizen. He believes himself to be living in a world in which he is spied upon, plotted against, betrayed, and very likely destined for total ruin. He feels that his liberties have been arbitrarily and outrageously invaded. He is opposed to almost everything that has happened in American politics for the past twenty years. He hates the very thought of Franklin D. Roosevelt. He is disturbed deeply by American participation in the United Nations, which he can see only as a sinister organization. He sees his own country as being so weak that it is constantly about to fall victim to subversion; and yet he feels that it is so all-powerful that any failure it may experience in getting its way in the world—for instance, in the Orient—cannot possibly be due to its limitations but must be attributed to its having been betrayed. He is the most bitter of all our citizens about our involvement in the wars of the past, but seems the least concerned about avoiding the next one. While he naturally does not like

Soviet communism, what distinguishes him from the rest of us who also dislike it is that he shows little interest in, is often indeed bitterly hostile to such realistic measures as might actually strengthen the United States vis-à-vis Russia. He would much rather concern himself with the domestic scene, where communism is weak, than with those areas of the world where it is really strong and threatening. He wants to have nothing to do with the democratic nations of Western Europe, which seem to draw more of his ire than the Society Communists, and he is opposed to all "give-away programs" designed to aid and strengthen these nations. Indeed, he is likely to be antagonistic to most of the operations of our federal government except Congressional investigations, and to almost all of its expenditures. Not always, however, does he go so far as the speaker at the Freedom Congress who attributed the greater part of our national difficulties to "this nasty, stinking 16th [income tax] Amendment." . . .

One of the most urgent questions we can ask about the United States in our time is the question of where all this sentiment arose. The readiest answer is that the new pseudo-conservatism is simply the old ultra-conservatism and the old isolationism heightened by the extraordinary pressures of the contemporary world. This answer, true though it may be, gives a receptive sense of familiarity without much deepening our understanding, for the particular patterns of American isolationism and extreme right-wing thinking have themselves not been very satisfactorily explored. . . .

Elmer Davis, seeking to account for such sentiment in his recent book, "But We Were Born Free," ventures a psychological hypothesis. He concludes, if I understand him correctly, that the genuine difficulties of our situation in the face of the power of international communism have inspired a widespread feeling of fear and frustration, and that those who cannot face these problems in a more rational way "take it out on their less influential neighbors, in the mood of a man who, being afraid to stand up to his wife in a domestic argument, relieves his feelings by kicking the cat." This suggestion has the merit of both simplicity and plausibility, and it may begin to account for a portion of the pseudo-conservative public. But while we may dismiss our curiosity about the man who kicks the cat by remarking that some idosyncrasy in his personal development has brought him to this pass, we can hardly help but wonder whether there are not, in the backgrounds of the hundreds of thousands of persons who are moved by the pseudo-conservative impulse, some commonly

shared circumstances that will help to account for their all kicking the cat in unison. . . .

What I wish to suggest—and I do so in the spirit of one setting
forth nothing more than a speculative hypothesis—is that pseudo-
conservatism is in good part a product of the rootlessness and
heterogeneity of American life, and above all, of its peculiar
scramble for status and its peculiar search for secure identity.
Normally there is a world of difference between one's sense of
national identity or cultural belonging and one's social status.
However, in American historical development, these two things,
so easily distinguishable in analysis, have been jumbled together
in reality, and it is precisely this that has given such a special
poignancy and urgency to our status-strivings. In this country a
person's status—that is, his relative place in the prestige hierarchy
of his community—and his rudimentary sense of belonging to the
community—that is, what we call his "Americanism"—have been
intimately joined. Because, as a people extremely democratic in
our social institutions. we have had no clear, consistent and
recognizable system of status, our personal status problems have
an unusual intensity. Because we no longer have the relative
ethnic homogeneity we had up to about eighty years ago, our
sense of belonging has long had about it a high degree of un-
certainty. We boast of "the melting pot," but we are not quite
sure what it is that will remain when we have been melted
down. . . .

Status problems take on a special importance in American life
because a very large part of the population suffers from one of
the most troublesome of al status questions: unable to enjoy the
simple luxury of assuming their own nationality as a natural
event, they are tormented by a nagging doubt as to whether they
are really and truly and fully American. Since their forebears
voluntarily left one country and embraced another, they cannot,
as people do elsewhere, think of nationality as something that
comes with birth; for them it is a matter of *choice*, and an object
of striving. This is one reason why problems of "loyalty" arouse
such an emotional response in many Americans and why it is so
hard in the American climate of opinion to make any clear distinction between the problem of national security and the question
of personal loyalty. Of course there is no real reason to doubt
the loyalty to America of the immigrants and their descendants,
or their willingness to serve the country as fully as if their
ancestors had lived here for three centuries. None the less, they
have been thrown on the defensive by those who have in the
past cast doubts upon the fullness of their Americanism. Possibly

they are also, consciously or unconsciously, troubled by the thought that since their forebears have already abandoned one country, one allegiance, their own national allegiance might be considered fickle. For this I believe there is some evidence in our national practices. What other country finds it so necessary to create institutional rituals for the sole purpose of guaranteeing to its people the genuineness of their nationality? Does the Frenchman or the Englishman or the Italian find it necessary to speak of himself as "one hundred per cent" English, French or Italian? Do they find it necessary to have their equivalents of "I Am an American Day?" When they disagree with one another over national policies, do they find it necessary to call one another over national policies, do they find it necessary to call one another un-English, un-French or un-Italian? No doubt they too are troubled by subversive activities and espionage, but are their countermeasures taken under the name of committees on un-English, un-French or un-Italian activities? . . . (21)

Seymour Martin Lipsett, in his contributions to *The Radical Right* pins down the relationship between status politics and the politics of hate.

Any analysis of the role of political extremism in the United States must recognize the fundamental political forces operating under the varying historical conditions of American society. These forces may be distinguished by the terms *status politics* and *class politics*. Class politics refers to political division based on the discord between the traditional left and the right, i.e. between those who favor redistribution of income, and those favoring the preservation of the *status quo*. Status politics, as used here, refers to political movements whose appeal is to the not uncommon resentments of individuals or groups who desire to maintain or improve their social status.

In the United States, political movements or parties which stress the need for economic reform have usually gained strength during times of unemployment and depression. On the other hand, status politics becomes ascendant in periods of prosperity, especially when full employment is accompanied by inflation, and when many individuals are able to improve their economic position. The groups which are receptive to status-oriented appeals are not only those which have risen in the economic structure and who may be frustrated in their desire to be accepted socially by those who already hold status, but also those groups already possessing status who feel that the rapid social change threatens their own claims to high social position or enables previously lower status groups to claim equal status with their own.

. . . While on the one hand, the status-threatened old-family American tends to over-emphasize his identification with American conservative traditions, and thus be potentially or actually a supporter of the radical right, the new American, the minority ethnic, also is in strong need of asserting his status claims. For while the old American desires to maintain his status, the new American wishes to obtain it, to become accepted. This is particularly true for those members of the minority groups who have risen to middle or upper class position in the economic structure. These groups, having entered at the bottom, tend to view the status hierarchy as paralleling the economic ladder; they believe that one need only move up the economic scale to obtain the good things of the society. But as they move up economically, they encounter social resistance. There is discrimination by the old-family Americans, by the Anglo-Saxon against the minority ethnics.

The Boston Brahmins, for example, do not accept the wealthy Irish. As Joseph Kennedy, . . . once put it in reaction to the fact that the Boston press continually made reference to him as Irish: "I was born here, my children were born here. What the hell do I have to do to be an American?" All through the country, one can find ethnic groups, often composed of third and fourth generation Americans, who have developed their own middle and upper classes, but whom are still refused admittance into the social circles of Anglo-Saxon Protestants. One of the major reactions to such discrimination, as indicated earlier, is to become overconformists to an assumed American tradition. Since many members of these ethnic groups do not want to be defined as Europeans, they also tend to become isolationist, ultra-patriotic, and even anti-European. For them, as for the old American traditionalist, the positive orientation towards Europe of liberals, of moderate conservative internationlists, creates a challenge to their basic values and to their rejection of Europe. Thus the status-insecure old-family American middle class and the status-striving minority ethnics both arrive at similar political positions. . . . Prosperity magnifies the status problem by challenging the economic base of the older groups, and accentuating the claim to status of the emerging ones. As a general hypothesis I would suggest that the supporters of the radical right in the 1950's come disproportionately from both the riding ethnic groups and those old-family Americans who are oriented toward a strong identification with the past.

. . . The political consequences of status frustrations are very different from those resulting from economic deprivation, for while in economic conflict the goals are clear—a redistribution of income—in status conflict, there are no clear-cut solutions. Where there are status anxieties, there is little or nothing which a government can do. It is not surprising, therefore, that the political movements which have successfully appealed to status resentments have been irrational in character and have sought scapegoats which conveniently serve to symbolize the status threat. Historically, the most common scapegoats in the United States have been the minority, ethnic or religious groups. Such groups have repeatedly been the victims of political aggression in periods of prosperity, for it is precisely in these times that status anxieties are most pressing. . . . (22)

Daniel Bell, in his article, "The Dispossessed—1962," written for *The Radical Right*, analyzes the emergence of the extreme right-wing movement in terms of predisposing factors and events.

. . . The factors that precipitated the radical right into quick notoriety in early 1961 were the rancor of their attacks and the flash spread of the movement in so many different places. McCarthyism in the mid-1950's was never an organized movement; it was primarily an atmosphere of fear, generated by a one-man swashbuckle cutting a wide swath through the headlines. In some localities—in Hollywood, on Broadway, in some universities —individual vigilante groups did begin a drumbeat drive against Communists or former fellow-travelers, but by and large the main agitation was conducted in government by Congressional or state legislators, using agencies of legislative investigation to assert their powers. In contrast, the radical right of the 1960's has been characterized by a multitude of organizations that seemingly have been able to evoke and intense emotional response from a devoted following.

Three elements conjoined to attract public attention to the radical right. One was the disclosure of the existence of the John Birch Society, a secretive, conspiratorial group obedient to a single leader, Robert Welch, who argued that one could combat the methods of Communism only with Communist methods. Thus, membership lists were never disclosed, fronts were organized to conduct campaigns (such as the one to impeach Chief Justice Warren, which turned with heavy-handed jocularity into calls to "hang" him), and a symbol of patriotism was put forth in the name of an Army captain who had been shot in China by the Communists.

The second was the fashionable spread of week-long seminars of anti-Communist "schools," conducted by evangelist preachers who adapted old revivalist techniques to a modern idiom, which swept sections of the country, particularly the Southwest and

California. These schools promised to initiate the student into the "mysteries" of Communism by unfolding its secret aims, or unmasking the philosophy of "dialectical materialism." And third, there was the disclosure of the existence of extreme fanatic groups such as the Minutemen, who organized "guerilla warfare seminars," complete with rifles and mortars, in preparation for the day when patriots would have to take to the hills to organize resistance against a Communist-run America. Such fringe movements, ludicrous as they were, illustrated the hysteria that had seized some sections of the radical right. . . . (23)

Dr. Bell goes on to an appraisal of the Radical Right in terms of its current and ultimate impact on American life.

The distinctive theme of the radical right is that not only is Communism a more threatening force today than at any other time in the past forty years, but that the threat is as great domestically as it is externally. . . . In fact, so great is the preoccupation with the alleged domestic threat that only rarely in the press of the radical right is there any mention of Russia's military prowess, its scientific equipment, or its ability to propel intercontinental ballistic missiles. When such facts are raised, it is often asserted either that such strength is a sham or that whatever knowledge Russia has was "stolen" from the United States. . . .

The unwillingness of the radical right to recognize Russian military strength as a prime factor in the balance of terror, and the compulsive preoccupation with a presumed internal threat, can perhaps be clarified by a little understood psychological mechanism—the need to create "fear-justifying" threats in order to explain fright that is provoked by other reasons. . . . In short, the radical right, having a diffused sense of fear, needs to find some story of explanation to explain or justify that fear. One can deny the external reality and build up the internal threat through such psychological mechanisms. . . .

What the right wing is fighting in the shadow of Communism is essentially "modernity,"—that complex of attitudes that might be defined most simply as the belief in rational assessment, rather than established custom, for the evaluation of social change—and what it seeks to defend is its fading dominance, exercised once through the institutions of small-town America, over the control of social change. But it is precisely these established ways that a modernist America has been forced to call into question. . . .

Within this perspective, therefore, what are the prospects of the radical right? To what extent does it constitute a threat to democratic politics in the United States? Some highly competent political observers right off the radical right as a meaningful political movement. . . . Yet, given the severe strains in American life, the radical right does present a threat to American liberties, . . . Democracy, as the sorry history of Europe has shown, is a fragile system, and if there is a lesson to be learned from the downfall of democratic government in Italy, Spain, Austria and Germany, and from the deep divisions in France, it is that the crucial turning point comes, as Juan Linz has pointed out, when political parties or social movements can successfully establish "private armies" whose resort to violence—street fightings, bombings, the break-up of their opponents' meetings, or simply intimidation—cannot be controlled by the elected authorities, and whose use of violence is justified or made legitimate by the respectable elements in society.

In America, the extreme-right groups of the late 1930's—the Coughlinites, the German-American Bund, the native fascist groups—all sought to promote violence but they never obtained legitimate or respectable support. The McCarthyite movement of the early 1950's, despite the rampaging antics of its eponymous leader, never dared go, at least rhetorically, outside the traditional framework in trying to establish loyalty and security tests. The Birchers, and the small but insidious group of Minutemen, as the epitome of the radical right, are willing to tear apart the fabric of American society in order to instate their goals and they did receive a temporary aura of legitimacy from the conservative right.

Barbarous acts are rarely committed out of the blue. (As Freud says, first one commits oneself in words, and then in deeds). Step by step, a society becomes accustomed to accept, with less and less moral outrage and with greater and greater indifference to legitimacy the successive blows. What is uniquely disturbing about the emergence of the radical right of the 1960's is the support it has been able to find among traditional community leaders who have themselves become conditioned, through an indiscriminate anti-Communism that equates any form of liberalism with Communism, to judge as respectable a movement which, if successful, can only end the liberties they profess to cherish. (24)

THUNDER ON THE RIGHT
THE JOHN BIRCH SOCIETY

The rallying point for the Radical Right is, in the words of Alan Barth, "that proliferation of societies, leagues, committees, councils and crusades which propose to stop the clock—or, to turn its hands back to some easier, earlier time when men could move more readily and directly to achieve what they wanted." And of these, the John Birch Society is probably the best known. The logical successor to the nativist groups of the thirties and the McCarthy movement of the fifties, the John Birch Society embraces these, and yet by avoidance of the appearance of extremism, attracts a much broader base. The Society has been succinctly analyzed in an article, "The John Birch Society, Fundamentalism on the Right," by Professor Alan F. Westin, appearing in *Commentary* magazine in its issue of August, 1961.

What It Is and What It Advocates

However much factors like urbanization, the cold war, and status insecurities may have provided a new setting for native fundamentalists, a large and irreducible corps of such people has always existed in the United States. Unlike American liberals and conservatives—who accept the political system, acknowledge the loyalty of their opponents, and employ the ordinary political techniques—the fundamentalists can be distinguished by five identifying characteristics:

(1) They assume that there are always solutions capable of producing international victories and of resolving our social problems; when such solutions are not found, they attribute the failure to conspiracies led by evil men and their dupes.

(2) They refuse to believe in the integrity and patriotism of those who lead the dominant social groups—the churches, the unions, the business community, etc.—and declare that the American "Establishment" has become part of the conspiracy.

(3) They reject the political system; they lash out at "political" compromise as a betrayal of the fundamental Truth and as a circus to divert the people.

(4) They reject those programs for dealing with social, economic, and international problems which liberals and conservatives agree upon as minimal foundations. In their place, the fundamentalists propose drastic panaceas requiring major social change.

(5) To break the net of conspiracy they advocate "direct action," sometimes in the form of a new political party, but more

often through secret organization, push-button pressure campaigns, and front groups. Occasionally "direct action" will develop into hate-propaganda and calculated violence.

At various periods, the United States has experienced both left-fundamentalism (the Knights of Labor, the Wobblies, the Populists, the Communists, the Trotskyites, and the Wallace Progressives) and right-fundamentalism (the Know-Nothings, the Coughlinites, the Silver-Shirts, and America First). Today, right-fundamentalism spans a broad spectrum. At one pole, with its passionate thousands, is the "hate" right, led by the Conde McGinleys, Gerald L. K. Smiths, Admiral Crommelins, Father Terminellos, John Kaspers, and George Rockwells, who offer various combinations of anti-Semitic, anti-Catholic, and anti-Negro sentiment. These groups are thoroughly discredited in contemporary America, and the major problem they present is a matter of defining the line which our law should draw between deviant expression and hate-mongering or advocacy of violence. At the opposite pole is the semi-respectable right. Here we encounter a variety of different political and educational organizations including the Foundation for Economic Education, the Daughters of the American Revolution, the Committee for Constitutional Government, and the White Citizens' Councils of the South. Socially prominent figures belong to such groups, which are well-financed, often have connections with local and national major party factions, and exercise substantial lobbying influence. Their supporters and leaders may long to break with the two-party system and start a rightist party, but they are retrained by the knowledge that this would isolate them and thus diminish their present effectiveness.

The John Birch Society stands between these two poles. In the words of one of its chapter leaders in Louisville, Kentucky, it is a "middle-of-the-road right-wing organization." In order to get a precise picture of its ideology and tactics, I have examined every published word issued by the Society since its formation in 1958: the 1961 annotated edition of the *Blue Book of the John Birch Society,* its operating manual and theological fount; the monthly *Bulletins* which are sent to members and contain the agenda of activities (1960 issues of the *Bulletin* are available in a bound edition titled *The White Book of the John Birch Society*); those writings of Robert Welch which have been officially incorporated and reprinted by the Society (e.g., *The Life of John Birch, May God Forgive Us, A Letter to the South on Segregation*); and every issue of *American Opinion,* the monthly publication edited by Robert Welch for the Society.

Measured by its offiicial materials, the authenticated accounts of Welch's speeches, and public comments by members of the

Society's Council, the Society emerges as a pure-bred specimen of American right-fundamentalism.

(1) *Its image of world events and American politics is wholly conspiratorial.* In the July 1960 *Bulletin,* Welch explains that the "key" to the advance of world Communism "is treason right within our government and the place to find it is right in Washington." The danger, Welch says in the *Blue Book,* "is almost entirely internal." And it is "a certainty," he writes in *May God Forgive Us,* that there are "more Communists and Communist sympathizers in our government today than ever before." As January 1961, Welch was informing his supporters that "Communist influences are now in almost complete control of our Federal Government."

Each year since 1958, Welch and his "board of experts" have published a "scoreboard" rating all the nations of the world according to the "present degree of Communist influence and control over the economic and political affairs" of the country. In 1958, the United States was rated as 20-40 per cent under Communist control; in 1959, the United States went up to 30-50 per cent; and in 1960, the figure climbed to 40-60 per cent. (At that pace, we will reach the 80-100 per cent mark in 1964.) England's rating went from 20-40 per cent in 1958 to 50-70 per cent in 1960. Israel is presently rated as 40-60 per cent controlled; Egypt 80-100 per cent.

Everywhere, the Birchers advise, Communists are at the heart of events, even some events that might seem to less skilled observers remote from Kremlin direction. In an open letter to Khrushchev in 1958, Welch said "your hands played the decisive unseen part" in the run on American banks and their closing in 1933. It was the Communist-contrived recognition of the Soviets in 1933 that "saved them from financial collapse." The "very idea of American foreign aid was dreamed up by Stalin, or by his agents for him." The "trouble in the South over integration is Communist-contrived"; the Communists have invented a "phony 'civil rights' slogan to stir up bitterness and civil disorder, leading gradually to police-state rule by federal troops and armed resistance to that rule." The United States Supreme Court "is one of the most important agencies of Communism." The Federal Reserve system is a "realization" of "point 5" of the *Communist Manifesto,* calling for centralization of credit in the hands of the state. The purpose of proposed legislation requiring registration of privately-owned firearms is to aid the Communists in making "ultimate seizure of such by the government easier and more complete." Everywhere, Welch concludes, the Communists are winning: in "the press, the pulpit, the radio and television media, the labor unions, the schools, the courts, and the legislative halls of America."

All the above descriptions of conspiratorial trends have been cited from official Birch Society literature, what Welch calls the Society's "steps to the Truth." But the picture grows darker when one turns to the *Black Book*, or, as it is more commonly known, *The Politician*—the book-length "letter" which Welch circulated "privately" to hundreds of persons but which the Society has carefully rejected as an official document. *The Politician* is to the Society what Leninist dogma is to the Communist front groups in Western or neutralist nations— it is the ultimate truth held by the founder and his hard-core, but it is too advanced and too powerful to present, as yet, to the "masses" being led. In *The Politician*, Welch names names. President Roosevelt. Truman, and Eisenhower; Secretary of State John Foster Dulles; CIA Director Allen Dulles; Chief Justice Warren—all of these men are called knowing instruments of the Communist conspiracy.

It is worth noting that Eisenhower and his administration draw the strongest venom in *The Politician*, just as Social Democrats do in full-dose Communist literature. For Welch (a Taft supporter and McCarthy stalwart), the Eisenhower administration was a betrayal which could only have had Communists at its source. "For many reasons and after a lot of study," Welch writes, "I personally believe [John Foster] Dulles to be a Communist agent." "Allen Dulles is the most protected and untouchable supporter of Communism, next to Eisenhower himself, in Washington." Arthur H. Burns's job as head of the Council of Economic Advisers "has been merely a cover-up for Burns's liaison work between Eisenhower and some of his Communist bossess." "The chances are very strong that Milton Eisenhower is actually Dwight Eisenhower's superior and boss within the Communist Party." As for Dwight Eisenhower himself, Welch states unequivocally: "There is only one possible word to describe [Eisenhower's] purpose and actions. That word is treason." "My firm belief that Dwight Eisenhower is a dedicated, conscious agent of the Communist conspiracy," he continues, "is based on an accumulation of detailed evidence so extensive and so palpable that it seems to put this conviction beyond any reasonable doubt." Discussing what he terms Eisenhower's "mentality of fanaticism," Welch refuses to accept the idea that Ike may just be an "opportunistic politician" aiding the Communists. "I personally think he has been sympathetic to ultimate Communist aims, realistically willing to use Communist means to help them achieve their goals knowingly accepting and abiding by Communist orders, and consciously serving the Communist conspiracy for all of his adult life."

(2) *The Birchers impugn the integrity and patriotism of those at the head of the major social and economic groups of the nation.* In a supplement to the February 1961. *Bulletin.* Welch announced that "Communist influences" are "very powerful in the top echelons of our educational system, our labor-union organizations, many of our religious organizations, and of almost every important segment of our national life. Insidiously but rapidly the Communists are now reaching the tentacles of their conspiracy downward throughout the whole social, economic, and politcial pyramid." Thus, the National Council of Churches of Christ is Communist-minded, and from 3 to 5 per cent of the Protestant clergy have been actual Communists. "Treason," Welch further declares, "is widespread and rampant in our high army circles." The American Medical Association has been "took" and can no longer be depended upon for support in the fight against socialism. So too with the United States Chamber of Commerce, which has been preaching dangerously liberal and internationalist doctrines in its course on practical politics. (When Chamber leaders protested this slur, Welch replied that their outraged reaction was extactly like that of the State Deparment in the 1940's when charges of Communist infiltration were first raised.) The leadership of our universities, corporations, foundations, communications media—all are riddled with Communists, or "Commsymps" (a word Welch coined to avoid having to say whether a given person was a real party member or only a sympathizer).

Naturally, Welch and his colleagues are certain that these "Comsymp" elites are out to destroy him and his movement. References to persecution and images of martyrdom abound in Birch literature, ranging from incessant mention of how the patron said (Senator McCarthy) was driven to his death, to suggestions that Welch may be murdered one day by the Communists.

(3) *The Birchers are convinced that the Communists have gone so far in penetrating American politics that there is little hope in the existing political system.* In his letter to Khrushchev, Welch wrote that the Communists obviously intended to "maintain and increase [their] working control over both our major political parties." We cannot count on "politicians, political leadership or even political action." Though he advocates the nomination, on an American Party ticket, of Senator Barry Goldwater for President and J. Strom Thurmond for Vice President in 1964, Welch has warned his followers that even Goldwater

—the most "Americanist" figure around in politics at the moment —is "still a politician" and therefore not to be relied upon. Welch has also had some things to say about "Jumping Jack". Kennedy. According to Welch, the nation received "the exact Communist line . . . from Jack Kennedy's speeches, as quickly and faithfully as from the *Worker* or the *National Guardian*. . . ." And in 1959, Welch denounced the "Kennedy brat" for "finding the courage to join the jackals picking at the corpse of McCarthy."

A particularly revealing sample of Welch's sense of American political realities is found in his description of Eisenhower "steal" of the Republican nomination in 1952, one of the "dirtiest deals in American political history, participated in if not actually engineered by Richard Nixon." If Taft had not been cheated of the nomination, Welch predicted:

> It is almost certain that Taft would then have been elected President by a far greater plurality than was Eisenhower, that a grand rout of the Communists in our government and in our midst would have been started, that McCarthy would be alive today, and that we wouldn't even be in this mess. . . .

(4) *Most of the Birch Society's positive program consists of advocating the repeal of things or the removal of the nation from something or somewhere.* A partial list of the things that the Society describes as wicked, Communist, and dangerous includes: U.S. membership in the United Nations, the International Labor Organization, the World Health Organization, the International Trade Organization, and UNICEF; membership in GATT (the General Agreement on Trades and Tariffs); reciprocal trade agreements; the "useless and costly" NATO; "so-called defense spending"; all foreign aid; diplomatic relations with the Soviet Union and all other Communist nations; the National Labor Relations Act; social security; the graduated income tax; the Rural Electrification Administation, the Reconstruction wage and price controls; "forced integration"; "deliberately fraudulent" U.S. government bonds; the Federal Reserve system; urban renewal; fluoridation; metro government; the corporate dividend tax; the "mental health racket"; federal aid to housing; and all programs "regimenting" farmers.

Some items on this list may be opposed by conservatives or by liberals. But taken together, it adds up to a nihilist's plea for the repeal of industrialism and the abolition of international politics. Such a program can be called rational or even political only by people who do not know what those words mean.

(5) *Finally, the Birch Society advocates both "direct action" and "dirty tactics" to "break the grip of the Communist con-*

spiracy." Unlike those right-fundamentalist groups which have energetic leaders but passive memberships, the Birchers are decidedly activist. "Get to work or learn to talk Russian," is a slogan Welch recommends to his followers, and they are certainly hard at work. From national headquarters in Belmont, Massachusetts, Welch formulates a set of complementary national and local action programs, then issues them to members through directives in the *Bulletin* and contacts with chapter leaders. A mixture of traditional and fundamentalist techniques is prescribed. The local programs include infiltration of community organizations such as PTA ("to take them away from the Communists"); harassment of "pro-Communist" speakers at church meetings, political gatherings, and public forums; creation of local front groups (e.g., the Committee Agains Summit Entanglements, College Graduates Against Educating Traitors at Government Expense, the Committee to Impeach Earl Warren, and the Committee to Investigate Communist Influences at Vassar College); campaigns to secure endorsement of Birch positions and signatures for Birch petitions in all groups that Birch members belong to (e.g., veterans and busines organizations); letters and telephone calls to local public officals, leading citizens, and newspapers who support what the Society opposes or oppose the Society directly; monthly telephone calls to the local public library to make sure it has copies of the five right-wing books recommended by Welch every month.

The national campaigns are carelly pinpointed efforts. They range from letter-and postcard-writing to national advertising campaigns. In the past two years, Birchers have been told to: write the National Boy Scouts director and demand to know why the president of the National Council of Churches addressed their National Jamboree; insist personally and in writing each time a member flies American, United, or Eastern Airlines that they stock *Human Events* and *National Review* on their planes; write to *Newsweek* to protest a "pro-FLN Communist" story (the Society has a crush on Jacques Soustelle), to *Life* protesting the "glorification" of Charles Van Doren, and to the NBC network and the Purex Corporation for sponsoring a TV drama favorable to Sacco and Vanzetti; circulate petitions and write letters on the number one project of the moment, to impeach Chief Justice Warren and thereby "give the Communists a setback." Welch also sends out the copy for punchy postcards to be addressed to national political leaders. To cite instances in 1960 alone: to Ambasador Henry Cabot Lodge, Jr. at the UN, "Two questions, Mr. Lodge—Who Murdered Bang-Jensen? And Which Side are You On?"; to Secretary of State Christian Herter, "Castro is a

Communist. Trujillo is an anti-Communist. Whose Side are You On?"; and to President Eisenhower, on the eve of the scheduled summit conference, "Dear President Eisenhower—If you go, don't come back."

The last postcard stirred some protests from Society members, who felt that Welch's savage little message to the President was a bit too strong. Welch set them straight in the *Bulletin*: "It is one of our many sorrows that, in fighting the evil forces which now threaten our civilization, for us to be *too civilized* is unquestionably to be defeated." The Communists, he continued, want us to be "too gentle, too respectable . . . [but] this is not a cream-puff war . . . and we do mean business every step of the way." Welch admitted that the technique of planted and loaded questions and the disruption of meetings was a "dirty trick," but he still defended it as another vital tactic.

To stimulate compliance by members with the local and national efforts prescribed each month in the *Bulletin*, Welch has devised the MMM system, or "Member's Monthly Memos." These forms are filled out by the member detailing what he or she has done and including sundry observations on the "Americanist fight." They are then collected by the chapter leader and transmitted to Belmont. Welch and his staff, according to the *Bulletin*, spend much time going over the MMM's.

So far, the Birch Society has been successful in attracting to it some highly substantial figures in local communities—physicians, stockbrokers, retired military officers, lawyers, businessmen (particularly small and middle-sized manufacturers in the Midwest and South), and professionals, many of whom have become local chapter leaders and state coordinators. The Council of the Society is a veritable board of directors of right-fundamentalism: men like Colonel Lawrence Bunker, Cola G. Parker, T. Coleman Andrews, Clarence Manion, and Spruille Braden. Among the contributing editors and editorial advisory committee for *American Opinion* are J. B. Matthews, William S. Schlamm, Kenneth Colegrove, J. Braken Lee, Ludwig von Mises, Adolph Menjou, J. Howard Pew, and Albert C. Wedemeyer. In several communities, observers of the Society have noted a significant number of thirty-to-forty-year-olds joining the organization. Welch has stated that half of the Society's membership is Catholic, that there are some Jewish members, and that there are Negroes also —two segregated locals in the South and integrated chapters in the North.

Press reports suggest that most of the Society's members already had strong affiliations with other right-wing groups before the Birch Society was formed. What Welch hopes to do is build a one-million member organization by welding together the masses of right-fundamentalist joiners into the fighting educational and pressure arm of the John Birch Society. In the *Bulletin* and *American Opinion, Welch continually* offers flattering saltues to various right-wing groups, publications, and personalities, stressing that "Americanists" can work in several forums at once for the cause. In May 1961, for example, Welch listed two pages of "other anti-Communist groups" which he endorsed and urged Birchers to support. These included the American Coalition of Patriotic Societies, the American Council of Christian Laymen, the Cardinal Mindszenty Foundation, the Catholic Freedom Foundation, the Christian Crusade, the Freedom Club (of Los Angeles), Freedom in Action (Houston), the Intercollegiate Society of Individualists, the Network of Patriotic Letter Writers (Pasadena), and We, The People! (Chicago). In turn, Welch's appearances are often sponsored by such groups: the Freedom Club of Reverend James Fifield arranged his Los Angeles rally, and the Sons of the American Revolution sponsored his Houston appearance.

To a large extent, Welch's personal selflessness and his salesmanship have already made him a rallying point for the fundamentalist right, and no recent right-wing group comes to mind which has achieved so large and solid a dues-paying and working membership. In a world of Communist advances in Asia and Africa, pressures on Berlin, vast changes in the relation of white to colored populations throughout the world, the Birch Society has developed a thoroughly satisfying way for the thin-lipped little lady from Wichita or the self-made manufacturer of plumbing fixtures in North Carolina to work in manageable little daily doses against "the Communists." The cancer of the unquestioned international Communist menace and the surgery of local pressure on the PTA and public library—here is a perfect appeal for right fundamentalism. This highlights the fact that the Society's most successful efforts to date have not been on the national scene but on the "soft underbelly" of American democracy—those places where a minimum of pressure can often produce maximum terror and restrictive responses. Welch has stressed that school boards, city colleges, local businesses, local clergy, and similar targets are the ones to concentrate on. Above all Welch has brought *coordination* to the fundamentalist right —coordinated targets, coordinated meetings and rallies, and coordinated pressure tactics. "All of a sudden," the director of a Jewish Community Council in one city reflected, "the right wingers began to function like a disciplined platoon. We have had to contend with precision and saturation ever since."

What Are the Prospects?

If this is what the Society advocates and how it functions, what are its immediate and long-range prospects? In the short run, the Society has lost one of its most potent weapons—the element of secrecy. Those in local communities who felt the sting of Birch campaigns during 1959-61 report that it was the factor of surprise at these sudden fundamentalist pressures and the unawareness of their organizational source which threw them off balance. Now, however, the Society has been brought into public view. Its authoritarian character and extremist statements have been attacked in both liberal and conservative newspapers; by important Catholic, Protestant, and Jewish leaders; and by political figures as diverse as Richard Nixon, President John Kennedy, Attorney General Robert Kennedy, Representative Sam Rayburn, Senator Thomas E. Dodd, and even Senator Barry Goldwater himself. The fact that a prominent leader of the Society who had been chosen as Washington lobbyist for the American Retail Federation was hastily discarded in June by the Federation because of his Birch affiliation indicates that recent publicity has damaged the Society's claim to respectability. One Midwestern Congressman known for his open advocacy of right-wing movements felt it wise recently to seek out liberal leaders from his community and explain privately that he did *not* support the Birch movement. Increasingly those "solid" figures who joined the group when it was operating privately will have to face public disapproval of the Society, and this will probably cause some falling away among border-line conservatives.

In the longer perspective, however, there are three specific factors which deserve mention in assessing the Society's potential growth. The first is the authoritarian character of the group and the centralized control exercised by Robert Welch (a situation which has led Senator Goldwater to criticize Welch directly). According to the charter of the Society, Welch is the absolute leader; there is no accounting of dues or contributions; there is no representative process or democratic system for selecting programs or defining positions; and Welch has the power (which he has used) to expel any member or chapter for reasons sufficient to him, without right of hearing or appeal on the expulsion. This has produced widespread criticism of Welch as a "little Hitler" and the Society as a group run on fascist lines. However, Welch has stressed again and again that he doesn't expect any member to carry out a project which violates his conscience; and that the Society definitely opposes an "enforced conformity" within its ranks. The controls, Welch explains, are needed to prevent Communist infiltration of the Society (which he believes has already began or will certainly begin as the Society becomes more effective) and infiltration by hate-mongers. This blend of leader-principle and group self-protection has great appeal to right-fundamentalists and even to some right-wing conservatives. The authoritarian set-up makes fine ammunition for liberal and main-stream-conservative fire, but this is not likely to harm Welch a bit in his recruiting among fundamentalists.

A second factor is Welch himself. The fantastic allegations he has made in *The Politician*—even though the book has not been endorsed by the Council and is, indeed, repudiated by some members—have branded him as an unbalanced figure and convinced many staunch conservatives that Welch is a truly dangerous leader. The conservative Los Angeles *Times* recently did a thorough exposé of the Society and wrote a stinging editorial which read Welch out of the conservative camp. Out of self-defense, Republicans in California joined in with the *Times* (especially in condemning Welch's attacks on Eisenhower), for the Birchers were proving so effective in pulling the Republican party to the far right that some counterattack was felt to be essential. Welch himself has been highly equivocal about *The Politician*. He insists that it was a "private" letter and never published, though he does not deny its authenticity. In the May 1961 issue of the *Bulletin*, he alludes to "questions or criticism from some of our most loyal members" relating to *The Politician*. To these, he replies that "the considerations involved in connection with many such matters are varied, over-lapping, involved, and with too many ramifications to be explained in short compass. There are even times when, for reasons of strategy, we take an oblique approach to a specific objective, and fully to explain every step of our course would seriously handicap our effectiveness." Having decided not to say anything at all, Welch assured members that if he "could give . . . the whole background of events" then objections might turn into approval, and with this, he dropped the subject of his *magnum opus*.

Those members and leaders of the Society who find anything to criticize in *The Politician* (and many have fully endorsed the charges it featured) have stressed that Welch is entitled to his personal views and that their disagreement with him on Ike or the two Dulles brothers indicates how free and diverse the Society is.

In all probability Welch's talents as an organizer, salesman, proselytizer, and unifier of right-wing ranks outweigh (for the right-wing aristocracy) his tactical blunder in *The Politician*,.

Since he controls the Society fully, he is not likely to be replaced, and, indeed, there is no indication that an acceptable replacement is available either in the Society or outside it. As long as he heads the Society, however, *The Politician* will severely limit his credibility outside fundamentalist strongholds.

A third factor relating to the Birch Society's immediate prospects is the question of anti-Semitism. Repeated charges have been made that the Society is a genteel endorser of anti-Semitic persons and literature. Welch has recommended to his members such anti-Semitic publications Russell Maguire's *American Mercury* and Merwin K. Hart's *Economic Council Newsletter*. Hart—who often talks about a conspiracy of "Zionists and their confederates" controlling America and whose organization was described by a Congressional committee investigating lobbying as one which relies on "an ill-concealed anti-Semitism"—is presently leader of the Birch Society's Manhattan Chapter No. 26. In addition, such openly anti-Semitic spokesmen as Conde McGinley have rushed to endorse the Birch Society. In the March 15, 1961 issue of *Common Sense*, McGinley wrote: "Inasmuch as we have received many inquiries from all over the United States regarding the John Birtch Society, we want to go on record. We believe this to be an effective, patriotic group, in good hands."

On the other hand, Welch has always appealed to all religions, has urged Jews to join the Society, and has warned that it is a "Communist tactic to stir up distrust and hatred between Jews and Gentiles, Catholics and Protestants, Negroes and Whites." Much of the April 1961 issue of his *Bulletin* is devoted to a discussion of the allegation that the Society is anti-Semitic, and what Welch has to say there is well worth close examination.

He opens by noting that "the most vicious" charges leveled against him have come from "such notorius anti-Semites as Lyrl Clark Van Hyning (*Women's Voice*) and Elizabeth Dilling (the *Dilling Bulletin*) on the grounds that my various committees and supporters are nothing but a 'bunch of Jews and Jew-kissers.' . . ." He then cites the names of Jewish members of the society such as Willi Schlamm, Julius Epstein, Morrie Ryskind, the late Alfred Kohlberg, and Rabbi Max Merritt, and indicates that it has been endorsed by the American Jewish League Against Communism (a Jewish right-fundamentalist group). Next, Welch explains that he probably has "more good friends of the Jewish faith than any other Gentile in America." When he was in the candy manufacturing business in Massachusetts, he recalls, he had many Jewish customers; he drank coffee in their kitchens at midnight, borrowed money from them and lent them money in return, and engaged in every kind of business and social activity with Jews.

Turning to some specific accusations, Welch admits that he used a pamphlet by Joseph Kamp as a source for his book, *May God Forgive Us,* and also paid Kamp a hundred dollars to go through *The Life of John Birch* to find errors. This was in 1954. But later, he says, he became "aware of both the fact and the weapon of anti-Semitism in America, and I wanted nothing further to do with Kamp after the 1954 contact, but he adds that he still simply doesn't know enough to say whether Kamp is really anti-Semitic.

Welch goes on to relate that a person who had been trying to convert one local chapter into "a hotbed of anti-Semitism" was dropped from the Society, and he pledges that the Society will never become a haven for anti-Semitic feeling "so long as I am directing its policies." After several additional paragraphs explaining why no member of the Jewish faith can also be a Communist (and pointing out that Karl Marx was "probably the most vicious anti-Semite of all times"), Welch concludes with the following warning:

> There is only one real danger in the charge of anti-Semitism today, to the man who actually is not anti-Semitic. It is that the utter (and in some cases malicious) unfairness of the charge may cause him to react with anger against Jews in general, and then begin to let some of his feeling creep into his writings or his speeches. That brings on even more vitriolic attacks, with a few more straws to support them. And so the development continues until the man in question winds up actually becoming violently anti-Semitic. And he seldom realizes that this was the Communist game and purpose all along of which the majority of Jews who innocently helped the Reds to implement it were as unaware and innocent as the ordinary Methodist who supports the National Council of Churches. And many an anti-Communist fighter of great promise in America has had his career ruined and his effectiveness destroyed by letting himself fall into that carefully prepared trap.

This will never hapen to him, Welch declares; to his "thousands of Jewish friends" he pledges, "I shall remain your friend, no matter what happens. . . ."*

All evidence available at the moment suggests the presence of a certain ambivalence in the Birch Society on the matter of anti-Semitism. Welch himself seems to be personally without bias toward Jews, and he wants the Society to reflect this posi-

---

*One other bit of information bearing on Welch's attitude is that he has been consistently anti-Nasser, viewing the Arab nationalists as aiding the Communists in gaining control of the Middle East.

tion. Yet there is no doubt that some local leaders and members are well known anti-Semites. With one after another of the rabbinical associations and major Jewish civic groups speaking out in complete condemnation of Welch and his movement, there will be rising pressures to respond to the "Jewish attacks." Probably, Welch will continue to allow some light flirtation with the more sophisticated anti-Semitic spokesmen. But it is a testimony to American maturity and the activities of Jewish defense agencies that open anti-Semitism is seen as a dead end today for any "middle-of-the-road right-wing organization."

One final aspect of the Society should be noted. Welch's writings have a remarkable combination of fantastic allegation and sweet reasonableness. Along with his proposals advocating drastic action against the Communist agents all over America will go reminders to be polite while making menacing telephone calls to local officials, to exercise self-restraint when attacked unfairly, and to take no action which violates "moral principles." "It is a major purpose of the John Birch Society," he often explains, one "never to be overlooked by its members, to help in every way we can—by example as well as precept—to restore an abiding sense of moral values to greater use as a guide of conduct for individuals, for groups, and ultimately for nations." If there are some right-fundamentalists to whom this sort of passage sounds a bit like the National Council of Churches, the total blend of warm-hearted, main-street vigilantism is still appealing to the majority of Welch's followers.

Whatever the specific prospects for the Birth Society—and I consider them unhapily bright—the 1960's will surely be years of expansion for the fundamentalist right in this country. Several things point toward that conclusion.

First, this will be a decade of immense frustration for American foreign policy. We will witness increased neutralism among the new nations; increased militancy among the non-white peoples over questions of color; constant military and scientific pressures from the Russians and, soon, the Chinese Communists; diminished American influence in the United Nations; greater conflict in Latin America; and continued outlays of foreign assistance which do not "buy loyalties" or "deliver votes" on critical issues. If the United States can simply prevent these situations from exploding, most informed students of diplomacy would think we had done well. But cutting losses inflicted by the stagnant 1950's and preparing hopeful future positions is not going to appeal to the right-fundamentalist masses (or the frantic pacifist variety on the left either). The right is unshakable in its faith in unilateral solutions and its belief that each loss for America can be traced to a Communist agent or "Comsymp" in the CIA, at the New York *Times,* in the Cathedral of St. John the Divine, or at the Yale Law School. And the inescapable strategic retreats of the early 1960's (Laos is a good example) will lend fuel to the fires on the right.

Second, the domestic racial issue also poses a serious threat of a rise in right-fundamentalism. In the 1960's, the struggle for Negro equality will move increasingly into areas outside the South. Lower-middle-class and middle-class resentments against Negro neighbors and Negro competitors are found to increase. The crescendo of Negro militancy and the spreading use of government power to enforce civil rights will peel away the already thinned layers of toleration in many sectors of the Northern and Western population. In this area of public policy, groups like the Birch Society—which are not explicitly anti-Negro but oppose compulsory integration—have a promising position, and the reservoirs of white hostility, unless carefully and wisely channelled by both white and Negro liberal leaders, could fill the well of the fundamentalist right to overflowing.

Third, there exists the distinct possibility of an unprecedented coalition of Catholic and Protestant right-fundamentalists in the 1960's. Only those who know little about the history of American Catholicism would assume that this is a monolithic community. Yet many factors suggest that the 1960's may see an even deeper division of American Catholics into warring ideological factions that has obtained at any time in the past. Already some influential Catholics are complaining bitterly that President Kennedy has joined the "Liberalist Establishment," that he has been "selling out" Catholic Church interests, and that the Administration of the first Catholic President may go down in history as the "softest on Communism." This is far from the dominant view among American Catholics. Indeed, it may represent the last thrashing of the old, super-loyalist element in the American Catholic community—a group which will be goaded to extremism by the sight of an a-clerical, literate, sophisticated Catholic liberal in the White House. Under these conditions, and with the magic memory of Joseph McCarthy to help bridge the chasm of the Reformation, the fundamentalist Protestants and the fundamentalist Catholics may enter into an alliance (possibly inside the Birch Society). (25)

It is interesting to observe that while the Radical Right attracts to its banner the old-line hate elements, these are far from prominent in the movement. In fact, they are virtually a source of embarrassment to the effort to attract as wide and diversified a following as possible. The intolerance characteristic of the movement is ideological rather than ethnic, although the very authoritarian personality which responds to the Radical Right is demonstrably capable of prejudice. Nevertheless, the playing down of ethnic bigotry has created a phenomenon referred to as "transtolerance," in which, for example, a McCarthy will allege that hostility of liberal elements to a Roy Cohn is the result of anti-Semitism. The operation of transtolerance is almost wittily detailed by Peter Viereck in his article, "The Revolt against the Elite," apearing as one of the selections in *The Radical Right.*

. . . Manifestations of ethnic intolerance today tend to decrease in proportion as ideological intolerance increases. In sharp contrast, both bigotries previously used to increase together.

If sociologists require a new term for this change (as if there were not enough jargon already), then at least let it be a brief, unponderous term. I would suggest the word "transtolerance" for this curious interplay between the new tolerance and the new intolerance. Transtolerance is ready to give all minorities their glorious democratic freedom—provided they accept McCarthyism or some other mob conformism of Right or Left. I add "or Left" because liberals sometimes assume conformism is inevitably to the Right. Yet "Right" or "Left" are mere fluctuating pretexts, mere fluid surfaces for the deeper anti-individualism (anti-aristocracy) of the mass man, who ten years ago was trying to thought-control our premature anti-Communists as "warmongers" and who today dams them as "Reds" and who ten years from now, in a new appeasement of Russia, may again be damning them as "Wall Street warmongers" and "disloyal international bankers."

Transtolerance is the form that xenophobia takes when practiced by a "xeno." Transtolerant McCarthyism is partly a movement of recent immigrants who present themselves (not so much to the world as to themselves) as a two hundred per cent hate-the-foreigner movement. And by extension: Hate "alian" ideas. Transolerance is also a sublimated Jim Crow: against "wrong" thinkers, not "wrong" races. As such, it is a Jim Crow that can be participated in with a clear conscience by the new, non-segregated flag-waving Negro, who will be increasingly emerging from the increased egalitarian laws in housing and education. In the same way it is the Irishman's version of Mick-baiting and a strictly kosher anti-Semitism. It very sincerely champions against anti-semites "that American Dreyfus, Roy Cohn"; simultaneously, it glows with the same mob emotions that in all previous or comparable movements have been anti-Semitic. The final surrealist culmination of this new development would be for the Ku Klux Klan to hold non-segregated lynching bees.

At the same moment when America fortunately is nearer racial equality than ever before (an exciting gain, insufficiently noted by American-baiters in Europe and India), America is moving further from liberty of opinion. "Now remember, boys, tolerance and equality," my very progressive schoolma'am in high school used to preach, "come from cooperation in some common task." If Orwell's 1984 should ever come to America, you can guess what "some common task" will turn out to be. Won't it be a "team" (as they will obviously call it) of "buddies" from all three religions" plus the significantly increasing number of Negro Mc-Carthyites, all "cooperating" in the "common task" of burning books on civil liberties or segregating all individualists of "all three" religions? (26)

The Viereck observations bring this anthology to a close on a note of satire and science fiction, with a dash of cynicism. It is perhaps inevitable that in a work dedicated to "that other tradition" in American life—the tradition of hate—cynicism as to our basic democracy should emerge. I would not want to close this volume on such a negative note. It is not merely a cliche to say that "the price of liberty is eternal vigilance." It is to speak a truism—and to confirm the reality that the two traditions are ever in contention with one another—and that if the passion or zeal or watch on our liberties is relaxed, then freedom must perish.

Certainly, in perusing the collection of writings in this volume, the reader must be impressed by the strong psychological orientation given to phenomena which are generally embraced as "social" or "political science." It is perhaps in the practical application of psychology to these problems, that truly scientific disciplines of human relations can be forged—and more important, that answers to the problems of hate, bigotry, intolerance and repression of liberty may be found. Facing the problems squarely and accepting that frustrations, anxieties, insecurities, jealousies and the like are the warp and woof of the tradition of hate may go a lot further than hiding behind shibboleths like melting pot," and "tolerance," and "botherhood weeks," and pretending that bigotry is an anomaly in a democratic society. It is a basic precept of psycho-analysis that when the patient is finally brought to see his problem, he stands a better chance of being cured. Perhaps, mass therapy can help us see our ills, and by seeing them, cure them. For it is an unhappy paradox of our society that we can bridge the distance to the heavens, but cannot bridge the distance between the hearts of men.

REFERENCES — PARTS II, III

(1)   Battelheim, B. and Janowitz, M., *Dynamics of Prejudice,* Studies in Prejudice" Series, (Harper & Bros., 1950) p. 1

(2)   Ackerman, N. W. and Jahoda, M., *Anti-Semitism and Emotional Disorder,* "Studies in Prejudice" Series, (Harper & Bros., 1950), p. 25

(3)   Fineberg, S. A., *Punishment without Crime,* (Doubleday & Co., Inc., 1949), p. 13

(4)   *Ibid,* pp. 11-12, 14, 17-24

(5)   *Op cit supra, Dynamics of Prejudice, pp.* 27-40

(6)   Sherif, Muzafer, "Experiments in Group Conflict," SCIENTIFIC AMERICAN, Nov., 1956

(7)   Lowenthal, L and Guterman, N., *Prophets of Deceit,* "Studies in Prejudice" Series, (Harper & Bros., 1949), pp. 13-14, 15-19

(8)   *Ibid,* pp. 6-10

(9)   *Ibid,* pp. 118-134

(10) *Ibid,* pp. 1-4; 159-160

(11) Wolfe, Ann G., "Why the Swastika?" (American Jewish Committee, 1962), pp. 8-35

(12) Caplovitz, D. and Rogers, C., "Swastika, 1960," (Anti-Defamation League, 1963)

(13) Anti-Defamation League, "George L. Rockwell, U. S. Nazi" FACTS, Vol. 15, No. 2, Oct., 1963

(14) American Jewish Committee, "Report on the Black Muslims," FOR YOUR INFORMATION, August, 1963

(15) Fineberg, S. A., "Quarantining the Bigot" (American Jewish Committee, 1962)

(16) Clark, Kenneth B., *The Negro Protest* (Beacon Press, 1963), Interview with Rev. Martin Luther King, pp. 39-42

(17) Anderson, Margaret, "The Negro Child Asks: Why?", N. Y. TIMES MAZAGINE, Dec. 1, 1963

(18) Baldwin, James, *The Fire Next Time* (Dial Press, 1963)

(19) *Ibid,* p.

(20) Hacker, Andrew, "What Kind of Nation Are We?" N. Y. TIMES MAGAZINE, Dec. 8, 1963

(21) Hofstadter, Richard, "The Pseudo-Conservative Revolt," *The Radical Right* (Doubleday a Co., Inc., 1963), pp. 63-70, 74-75

(22) Lipsett, Seymour M., "The Sources of the Radical Right," *The Radical Right, op cit supra,* pp. 260-261

(23) Bell, Daniel, "The Dispossessed," *The Radical Right, op cit supra,* pp. 3-4

(24) *Ibid.,* pp. 10-12

(25) Westin, Alan F., "The John Birch Society, Fundamentalism on the Right," COMMENTARY, August, 1961

(26) Viereck, Peter, "The Revolt against the Elite," *The Radical Right, op cit supra,* pp. 140-141

APPENDIX

The Fright Peddlers*

by

Hon. Thomas H. Kuchel

of California

Mr. President, the American people are keenly aware of the grave and evil hazards to our freedom and to our way of life which international communism is eternally dedicated to destroy.

Aside from a relative handful of traitorous zealots in the ranks or clutches of the Communist Party, we—all of us in this land—are unalterably committed to deter and, if necessary, to combat and defeat any aggression, Communist or otherwise, against us or our free friends, who, like us, propose to keep our freedom.

I rise today to speak of another danger we confront, not as dread or as foreboding, but equally offensive and evil to all reasonable, rational, free American citizens.

It is the danger of hate and venom, of slander and abuse, generated by fear and heaped indiscriminately upon many great Americans by another relative handful of zealots, in the ranks or clutches of self-styled "I am a better American than you are" organizations.

It results from a strange intellectual strabismus which professes to see our Government crawling with Communists and which, abandoning the processes of reason, pours its spleen upon anything or anybody which does not meet its own queer and puzzling dogmas.

Mr. President, in every day's deluge of mail at my office which sometimes means as many as 5,000 letters, telegrams, and postcards— there are generally a hundred and even two hundred letters which I describe simply as "fright mail."

Most of my colleagues receive such mail and most of them refer to it in much stronger terms. Coming from the most populous State in our Union, California, I think it is safe to say I get as much as anybody.

It is difficult enough attempting to answer thousands and thousands of letters which seek 15 answers to 15 questions on complicated foreign and domestic policies and issues—and by tomorrow at the latest.

Many times, the only economically and mechanically feasible way to reply is to send printed statements, which are then often returned in disgust because I have not answered with a long, personal letter.

But, Mr. President, that is a minor problem compared to what to do about the "fright mail."

Excerpted from a speech delivered in the Senate of the United States, May 2, 1963, as reported in the Congressional Record.

I know this is a matter which many of my colleagues have given a lot of thought to privately, but, so far as I know, no one has discussed publicly.

I cheerfully admit that I have, in the past, attempted to reply calmly and factually to "fright mail," mustering all the reason and reserve I could summon.

Yet, I have found over the years that this is not quite the answer.

For most fright mail writers will come right back a week later, terrified about something else, urgently stating that they do not believe me—and that I am either misinformed or worse. Sometimes, they darkly insinuate that treason has prompted the reply they have received.

Treason. I still cannot believe my eyes when I stare at the ugliest word in the American lexicon tossed about in a letter as casually as the "Dear Senator" salutation which opens it. Indeed, I was once charged with treason by a correspondent who then closed his letter a few words later with "Respectfully yours."

Treason. The most heinous crime on the American books. And not always scrawled illiterately on a scrap of a paper bag, but often typed meticulously on embossed paper.

In recent months, I have been casually accused of ignorance or of a desire to sell my country down the river because I have said for example, that it not only seemed untrue on its face, but was demonstrably untrue, that thousands and thousands of Chinese Communist troops were poised on the Mexican border for an attack on California.

It not only seemed untrue on its face, but was demonstrably untrue that such-and-such American or free world leader—44 of them in all—is a Communist agent. The gallant Eisenhower is a favorite target for their contemptible slime.

What new and frightening charge tomorrow's mail will bring, I cannot begin to anticipate.

But I do want to disclose the two latest and intertwined "frights"—and analyze them in detail—by quoting in its entirey a typical letter I received in recent days.

The letter, on good stationery and carefully typed, comes from a constituent who lives high in the Berkeley Hills in California. It is somewhat mild in its intimations of treason, but otherwise is sadly typical. It reads as follows:

DEAR SENATOR KUCHEL: Thanks for your reply of March 9 regarding the Disarmament Agency.

I do not accept your statement that I have been the victim of misinformation. It is the other way around. Either you do not know what you have voted for in Public Law 87-297, or you are a traitor to the United States.

I would suggest you get in touch with Mr. Theodore Jackman, box 10188, Greenville, S.C. He is an expert on this subject. I had the pleasure of hearing him here in Berkeley a few days ago. Undoubtedly, he will be more than glad to come and talk with you about United Nations control over the United States of America, disarmament, and so forth.

Right at the present time, the U.S. Army is conducting operations in Georgia — Operation Moccasin — which many citizens over the country believe is a prelude and a training exercise for the takeover of the United States in the very near future, under United Nations authority. Of course, due to the large protest from citizens, the Army is denying everything.

Senator Kuchel, you better study up on what's going on. You have gone on record to me that I am under a misapprehension that we are being unilaterally disarmed. If this country is taken over by the United Nations, I will personally label you a traitor.

You better study up on what's going on in this country.

Sincerely yours,

Mr. President, note carefully the language, typical of the fright letter. The writer is convinced, utterly convinced. There is no room for doubt. Of course, this is happening, he says; and, of course, that is happening, he says. Because "he knows." And how did he find out? And how, if it is possible, can we reach him with simple truth?

First, let us look at what is the simple truth.

Here is an editorial from the Claxton (Ga.) Enterprise, a weekly newspaper published in the area where Operation Water Moccasin was held. It is entitled "Fear of Snakes."

It reads as follows:

A national furor has been raised over the Army exercise recently underway here, known as Water Moccasin III. Our office has received numerous letters from such places as Richmond, Va.; Savannah; New Orleans; and Minneapolis—all expressing a grave dread over the operation.

Evidently a lot of folks are scared of snakes, and in their sick minds anything with the name of a snake conjures up visions of a viper or a maneating reptile that sets them off on weird fantasies that defy description.

One Congressman went so far as to suggest that the United States was training "barefooted Africans as guerrilla warriors," to be used to subjugate other African nations.

Another had it figured that the United Nations was sending in foreign troops to be trained to overthrow our Government. Another decided we were being trained in how to surrender our cities to insurgents.

Still another imagined all of this area being "invaded by hordes of Mongolians" who were overrunning the entire area.

It is fantastic what the human mind can dream up over the simple statement that a few foreign students will act as observers in the operation. We were in almost daily contact with an English major and an Italian police officer. We also were visited by an Army team that had a Turkish officer as an observer. But we missed out on the "hordes of foreign Communists."

Some of the statements we have read amount to hysteria, the result of a sick mind, carried away by the self-induced hallucinations. Our experience with the people involved directly in the operation left us with the feeling that we were taking part in some important training that may one day aid our Nation in its struggle for world peace against a foe that uses all sorts of unorthodox tactics. We are glad to know that we have people in our Armed Forces with the ability and training that these men showed during our observation of this operation.

We look forward to Operation No. IV, but we suggest that the Army change the name to Primrose Path IV—or Azalea Trail or some such title—Water Moccasin IV seems to make people dream bad dreams, and act like dope addicts.

The editorial demonstrates, rather savagely, but correctly, I think, the irrational frenzy of my correspondent's claims about Operation Water Moccasin, alleged Army subversion and United Nations take-over of the United States.

I shall send my frightened constituent a copy of it. But will it really convince him? Perhaps, perhaps not. The Claxton, (Ga.) Enterprise could be some clever sort of Communist front, my constituent may suspect.

But what is really frightening, is that I shall also have to send a copy of the editorial to several thousand similarly frightened Californians who have fallen hook, line and sinker for the Operation Water Moccasin "plot" and have asked me to do all I can to halt the operation, if I am a decent American, with any courage at all.

Just listen to some sample quotes from my mail on Operation Water Moccasin:

From Hermosa Beach:

Last night, in Los Angeles, I heard a talk by Mr. Theodore Jackman of Greenville, S.C., about a frightening military maneuver now being held in the State of Georgia, called Exercise Water Moccasin III. It is time Congress demands the facts about Exercise Water Moccasin III, the United Nations War Operations and NATO Operations.

From San Jose:

I am writing you this letter of protest, to the presence of foreign troops on American soil. That there are African Negro troops, who are cannables (sic), stationed in Georgia.

From Hollywood:

It is unconstitutional to quarter American troops in American homes, so how come these pagan, ruthless, brutal, Godless savages? Yes, we know of the U.N. plans to place Congolian and Congolese troops over our dear United States (the same kind of troops which ravished Katanga) if the U.N. can swing their damnable world police force plan, so undoubtedly these Moccasin troops are to be the same.

From Paradise:

From friends in the State of Georgia, I have a report that at this time there are 15,000 United Nations personnel from 15 countries, participating in what is known as Operation Water Moccasin.

From Westminster, near my home town:

I also understand there are oriental troops in Mexico at this moment waiting to "occupy" parts of California for their training.

From Berkeley:

The news has just broken, although there had been rumors for a week or more, that Georgia is the place for 16,000 African soldiers, being trained by the U.N. for guerrilla warfare. Complete with nose and ear rings. This time, the U.N., and our State Department, have gone too far.

From Sacramento, the capital of my State:

This morning on radio, over Mr. Beirpos' program, I heard the most fantastic thing I have ever heard. Water Moccasin—what is this secret fantastic thing going on in the Deep South. U.N. troops coming to America for some kind of a "war to invade America." Mr. Senator, these things are being said over the radio, and he would not say them if they were not true. He said, "it's a three-point program of the disarmament program."

From Los Angeles:

Water Moccasin—we are asking you to give us a report on what you are doing to protect our constitutional rights. Also repeal income taxes.

From Los Angeles:

I am greatly disturbed at the news of foreign troops on our soil, as in Water Moccasin III. I am convinced we must get out of the United Nations. There is no longer any doubt that it is dominated by the Communists.

From Los Angeles:

I have just heard about one of the most fantastic and truly frightening military maneuvers ever to be held in the United States. The Oxford, Miss., invasion and violence was illegal and completely unconstitutional. I feel the United Nations is responsible. The U.N. is no good. Let's get out of it—now. I'm still sick from the Katanga tragedy.

From Ontario:

These so-called war games are in reality a deceitful way of bringing in the troops that will be used to enforce United Nations law on U.S. citizens. What are you doing about this? Let's get out of the godless United Nations and kick it out of the United States of America.

Mr. President, just think of it—"cannibals stationed in Georgia," they have charged:

Pagan, ruthless, brutal godless savages, Mongolian and Congolese troops—world police plan. Fifteen thousand United Nations troops already here. Oriental troops in Mexico, waiting to occupy California. Sixteen thousand African troops, already in Georgia, with rings in their noses and ears. A war to invade America. A United Nations takeover. Integration, part of the disarmament program. Let's get out of the U.N. Investigate NATO.

And abolish income taxes, too—if, presumably, there is still time. Frightening is not the word for it. It is incredible.

It is incredible that so many Americans have been so cruelly swindled, and have allowed themselves to be so deceitfully duped, about a U.S. Army troop exercise instructing our soldiers in counter-guerrilla warfare—and witnessed, incidentally, by 124, not 15,000 or 16,000, foreign military officers from Canada, the Republic of China,

France, Great Britain, Guatemala, Indonesia, Iran, Italy, Japan, South Korea, Liberia, Pakistan, the Philippines, Spain, Thailand, Turkey, and Vietnam.

Now who and what whips up so many Americans to a state of frenzy and despair over such "conspiracies" as the U.S. Army's "sell-out to the United Nations" under the "direction of the Arms Control Agency."

The answers are not hard to find.

Two of my cited correspondents indicated a mysterious "Mr. Jackman, of Greenville, S.C.," has contributed.

Others—as do many of my frightened correspondents—enclosed for my edification another definite source—an ignorant, crude, and equally hysterical leaflet.

I ask unanimous consent that the leaflet be printed at this point in the Record.

There being no objection, the leaflet was ordered to be printed in the Record, as follows:

The United States Has No Army, No Navy, No Air Force

For doubting Thomases who think this statement is not true, Senate bill No. 2180 entitled "The Arms control and Disarmament Act" was approved by the House of Representatives as House bill 9118 and was signed into effect as Public Law 87-297 on September 26, 1961, by John F. Kennedy, President of the United States. This bill was prepared to expedite a plan already proposed at Geneva by our administration and State Department (see Publication No. 7277 for full particulars of its terms) to effect the "legal" connotation of disarmament.

The only thing that keeps our Army, Navy, and Air Force from being wiped out of existence is public opinion. At any time he chooses the President of the United States can now transfer our Army, Navy, and Air force (your husband, father, son, or brother) to the command of Eugene D. Kiseley (Russian) who is Secretary of the United Nations Security Council (World Police Force).

* * * * *

Attributed to secret agreement between Alger Hiss and Molotov confirmed by Trygvie Lie and U.S. State Department and verified by subsequent action, the Secretary of the United Nations Security Council (who is in command of the United Nations Military Secretariat (World Police Force) must always be a Russian.

Here is the record: 1946-49, Arkady S. Sobelov, U.S.S.R.; 1950-53, Konstantine Zinchenko, U.S.S.R.; 1953-57, Ilya Tchernyshev, U.S.S.R.; 1957-60, A. Dobrynin, U.S.S.R.; 1960-62, George P. Arkadev, U.S.S.R.; 1962—, Eugeny D. Kiselev, U.S.S.R.

Prepared by: United Societies of Methodist Laymen, Inc., Austin, Tex.

Mr. Kuchel. That is the leaflet. It is very much like the dozens of allegedly "patriotic" fliers and pamphlets and leaflets which pour into my office by the hundreds, attached to frantic, pleading, threatening messages, sometimes typed on the finest stationery.

It is distressing and disillusioning to find persons of normal educational attainments—or any educational level—falling hysterically and emotionally, without reservations, for the unadulterated venom spewed by out-and-out crackpots for paranoia and profit.

It is disgusting to find self-appointed saviors, whether infantile or cunning, preying profitably and psychotically on the fears of Americans in the name of anticommunism. Indeed, the ugly labors they perform are a service to the Kremlin itself. They seek to divide and too often succeed in dividing, our people, far better than any Communist agents could do.

Day in and day out, every Senator and every Government official I know works long, hard hours devoted to one primary mission:

To protect and promote the security, welfare, and best interests of one country and one country alone—the United States of America, a country all of us in this Chamber unashamedly revere.

Do these people really believe, I ask myself—and now I ask them—that a gigantic and incredible and unprecedented conspiracy has occurred in America in which the President and his Cabinet, 99 percent of the Congress, 99 percent of the Nation's journalists, and even the U.S. Army have all taken part to sell out our country?

Do they really believe further that this conspiracy is visible only to a small number of self-appointed saviors, such as Mr. Jackman?

If they do, the only reasonable reply I can give to them which they will understand is the honorable, 100 percent red, white, and blue expression: "Nuts."

Who, we might also ask, is this Mr. Jackman? He is simply the Reverend Theodore Jackman, an available speaker for the American Opinion Speakers Bureau, the "nationwide conservative speakers' exchange" run by the John Birch Society, whose major contribution to the security and welfare of the United States of America was to "unmask" Dwight Eisenhower as a traitor.

Speaking of that highly publicized organization, I digress for a moment to point out to my colleagues, who may not have heard, that the founder of the Birch group has recently revised the party line viewpoint on former President Eisenhower—at least somewhat.

According to newspaper reports, the latest reprints of the founder's memorable book "The Politician," now gives followers the following choice—

That he—Eisenhower—is a mere stooge, or that he is a Communist assigned the specific job of being a political front man.

But the ludicrous word from high up in the Birch councils on the late former Secretary of State John Foster Dulles, of course, remains: "I personally believe Dulles to be a Communist agent," the founder of the Birch Society continues to profess.

As Ripley said, "believe it or not."

But, returning to the leaflet, I have received so far more than 2,000 letters demanding abolition of the U.S. Arms Control Agency on the grounds cited in the leaflet. Indeed, several hundred constituents have sent to me this leaflet, or variations of it.

And the most depressing statistics of all are as follows:

Only four constituents have raised even the slightest doubt at all about the leaflet's validity—as only six even considered at all the possibility the Operation Water Moccasin fright was a hoax.

To the first few hundred constituents who wrote to me in panic that the Arms Control Act transfers our military to a Russian colonel, I observed mildly, they were victims of misinformation.

As my colleagues know, the forerunner of the U.S. Arms Control and Disarmament Agency was the Disarmament Administration, which was established under former President Eisenhower.

As my colleagues also know, strong support for the legislation to establish the Arms Control Agency was offered in testimony by such distinguished American leaders as Gen. Alfred M. Gruenther, former supreme commander of NATO; Gen. Lyman L. Lemnitzer, former Chairman of the Joint Chiefs of Staff and now supreme commander of NATO; Henry Cabot Lodge, my party's candidate for Vice President and a good American; Christian Herter, an able, dedicated American and Republican who serves the present administration as he did the last; and Robert Lovett, capable former Secretary of Defense.

Quoting from the report of the Committee on Foreign Relations of the U.S. Senate:

The (Arms Control) Agency is to be responsible, under the direction of the Secretary of State, for the acquisition of a fund of practical and theoretical knowledge about disarmament and is directed to conduct research in that field, to engage public or private institutions or persons for such studies, and to coordinate work in this field now being undertaken by other Government agencies in accordance with procedures to be established by the President.

And so, the Foreign Relations Committee of the U.S. Senate, composed of 11 Democrats and 6 Republicans, unanimously went on record in favor of the legislation.

I told my frightened constituents all of this.

I told them that the Arms Control Agency, endorsed by an overwhelming Senate vote of 73 to 14 in 1961, has no power to disarm our country; that the only authority it has is to conduct research on matters of arms control and the effect of any reduction in the level of armaments on various parts of our economy; that it reports to the President and does not act independently; that its function is merely to bring the best talent available so that our representatives and the President can deal effectively with arms control matters; and that no responsible public official believes in unilateral disarmament or disarmament without an effective means of inspection.

What was the result? More leaflets in return, even wilder than the first batch. Plus, new or renewed accusations as to what is prompting my answers.

Let me cite some of the further authority or proof they sent on:

I ask unanimous consent that the text of that creed be printed in the Record in full.

There being no objection, the leaflet was ordered to be printed in the Record, as follows:

The Handwriting on the Wall: Soon You Will
Be a Citizen of a Free America

The U.S. Congress has passed a law, No. 87-297, which established an office of dictator. This office to be filled by appointment, appointment by the President.

The appointee is not called dictator: he is called Director of Disarmament and Arms Control.

He shall give his orders to the Secretary of State and to the President; and they shall see that his orders are carried out.

There shall be no jurisdiction over him: neither by the President, nor by the Congress.

The Director shall collaborate with, and receive orders from Eugene Kiselev (Russian), the Secretary of the United Nations.

All the U.S. arsenals and conveyances; missiles, planes, tanks, and ships are through his orders to be placed at the disposal of the U.N. Secretary. Then, all military centers are to be dismantled, and all American military personnel discharged. But afterward, discharged Americans will be drafted by the United Nations, to serve it, in faraway places.

For your free America will be only a vassal state under the U.N. Uncle Sam cannot then move his finger, without permission from the United Nations. But Khrushchev and Russia always veto everything Uncle Sam requests. So then the U.N. will never favor the United States of America under any condition whatever.

Law 87-297 is operating. William C. Foster is the Director. Five atomic submarines, Polaris submarines have been given to the U.N. They have been definitely promised the U.N. by the President and Secretary McNamara, and airbases are frequently being dismantled. Law 87-297 makes Foster subject to no law, nor to any authoritative body.

You will not have your job, nor your home, neither your self. If your Congress is not awakened and caused to repeal Public Law 87-297 soon. It must be repealed very soon.

Let it be understood also, that there are deputy directors, and many more will be appointed. There will be these appointed officials over the entire country; and there will be no civil courts; neither any civil officers to appeal to: for these deputies' orders will supersede orders of all civil officers.

Sounds fantastic. Then listen: The U.N. did not help the liberty-loving people of Hungary. The U.N. stood by and watched the savage Communist hordes massacre the people of Hungary. The U.N. has harassed and caused atrocities to be committed upon the best and only great people of the Congo. The U.N. has never helped any liberty-loving people. The U.N. despises God. What is fantastic truly is that you are a personality: yet you do not know when you began to be: yet you have a destiny—and do not know where you are headed.

While you and I were overwhelmed with the many machinations of the modern era: the oneworlders, through their never-tiring kibitzers overwhelmed most of your Congress, and pressured them into surrendering your Government.

And who is William C. Foster, Director of Disarmament who has this great power? He is not only a member of the ruling power, the Council on Foreign Relations, but a Director of this Council. And who is Col. Marshall Sanders, U.S. Air Force—on active duty in the Air Force? He is the colonel assigned by the Air Force to serve this Council on Foreign Relations for 1 year. He is listed in the annual report of the Council on Foreign Relations for 1962-63 as Air Force research fellow. This should convince anyone who rules the country today.

(Send to the U.S. Flag Committee, Post Office Box 269, Jackson Heights, N.Y., for report on this Council on Foreign Relations, $1.)

Observe, there is that Russian colonel again, ever ubiquitous in "running the U.N.'s military operations" and getting ready to take over our Armed Forces, plus our jobs, our homes and our very selves.

It is simply impossible to take the time and energy to prove demonstrably the outright falsehood of every zany claim alleged by this leaflet—from the giving of atomic submarines to the U.N., to William Foster's supposedly being subject to no law.

But consider the key and most frightening plank in these leaflets—the charge that a Russian colonel is commanding or will command all of our military. Can its origin be found?

Yes, it can. It can be found word for word in, of all things, a stage play written in the early 1950's by one Myron C. Fagan, the national director of something in Hollywood called the Cinema Educational Guild. The play, titled "Thieves' Paradise," purported to show, in Fagan's own words:

Why we must get the United States out of the U.N.—and the U.N. out of the United States * * * (revealing) all the different phases of the diabolical plot—how the U.N. was a "Trojan Horse" sneaked into the United States to serve as a sanctuary for Red spies, saboteurs and American traitors * * * how it was to destroy our freedoms through "treaties" such as "genocide" and the "World Court" * * * to brainwash our youth through UNESCO and UNICEF, etc. * * * to drain us of our wealth through UNRAA, the Marshall plan, and our foreign aid give-aways * * * and finally to transform the United States into an enslaved unit of their Communist one-world government.

In a little green tract, titled "U.N. Tract No. I," from which I just read, and the Cinema Educational Guild quotes the following dialog from his play:

STEFAN. When they were setting up the U.N., Molotov and Alger Hiss made a secret agreement that the military chief of the U.N. was always to be a Russian, appointed by Moscow. The first such Chief was Arkady Sobelov.

RITA. I know—

STEFAN. But do you know why Moscow wanted that arrangement? (Rita shakes her head—Stefan explains gloatingly) To be prepared, if the U.N. would have to interfere in any Communist attempts to grab free states their man would have charge of that interference and—

RITA. (Breaks in—suddenly understands) and their man would be able to keep the Red commanders fully informed of all the plans and movements of the U.N. forces?

There it is. The basis for the charge that a Russian colonel is going to command our military.

Now, first, who is Myron Fagan, who discovered this vile plot so many years ago?

I quote briefly from portions of the 11th report of the State Senate Factfinding Subcommittee on Un-American Activities to the 1961 regular California Legislature:

We do not wish to impugn the sincerity of Mr. Fagan, but we do wish to make public the facts about his Cinema Educational Guild, and our opinion concerning the erroneous nature of many of the statements contained in its publications * * *. There are heavy evidences of anti-Semitism throughout many of the booklets and in many of the Fagan speeches * * *. Mr. Fagan may well be one of the Nation's outstanding experts on matters theatrical, but that does not necessarily qualify him as an expert in the field of countersubversive intelligence.

So there we have it. The daisy chain is complete.

And what the fright peddlers have handed down to one another, over the years, is a daisy of a whopper, a puerile and evil package of fright calculated to "scare the daylight" out of decent Americans.

This whopper has been debunked thoroughly over the years. Yet, here it is again. And not only in letters and leaflets. Let me quote from an item in the April 1963, issue of the despicable The Cross and The Flag, the anti-Semitic hate sheet of Gerald L. K. Smith:

U.N. Military Dictatorship

The world police force of the United Nations is run by a Communist carrying the title "Secretary of the U.N. Security Council." Since the beginning of the United Nations a Russian Communist has held this authoritative position of top U.N. military authority.

Below are the names of Soviet agents who have held this position to the exclusion of all other nations:

1946 to 1949: Arkady S. Sobelov, U.S.S.R.

1950 to 1953: Konstantine Zinchenko, U.S.S.R. Screened military directives to Gen. Douglas MacArthur during Korean police action.

1953 to 1957: Ilya Tchernyshev, U.S.S.R.

1957 to 1960: A. Dobrynin, U.S.S.R.

1960 to 1962: George P. Arkadev, U.S.S.R. Screened Congo-Katanga directives Eugeny D. Kiselev, U.S.S.R.

Or let me quote just a few paragraphs from a news item in the Long Beach, Calif., Independent, a metropolitan daily newspaper, of March 15, 1963:

The U.S. Government is trying to put all its Armed Forces under the command of a Russian general, John Rousselot told 600 persons in municipal auditorium Thursday night.

Rousselot, John Birch Society district governor for six Western States and former Congressman from California's 25th District, spoke on "Disarmament—Blueprint for Surrender."

This office (referring to Under Secretary for Security Council and Political Affairs) is held by a Russian general, he said, and if the United States turns over its armed forces to the U.N., the Russian general will command them.

Those fantastic charges, Mr. President, are false—completely false.

But when one, who was honored to be a Member of the Congress of the United States for 2 years—or even one who writes for an undisguised hatesheet, utters such a cry, there are Americans who listen and believe.

The facts are that our American Military Establishment is American and shall remain so. We joined the United Nations because we believe in and work for peace with justice in the world. Where the United Nations has sought to quell aggression, the United States has played its honorable role.

There is no Russian colonel, or general, or military or civilian individual who is "secretary of the United Nations" or "secretary of the U.N. Security Council."

Let the record be clear that there are 19 undersecretaries of the Security Council, of which 13 are filled by Americans or representatives of our allies and of which two are Soviet bloc nations.

None of them has anything to do with the command of any joint U.N. military operations. There is no world police force in the U.N. And, of course, no Soviet national ever gave Gen. Douglas MacArthur any orders.

How hysterical and idiotic can one get? I am afraid to answer, until I have seen tomorrow's mail.

Leaflets, of course, are not the only cause for hysteria.

Lunatic columnists, apostles of hate and fear on radio and television, and even loony letters to the editor provoke their share of fright mail.

The curious fact is that the fright peddlers, from the simple simpletons to the wretched racists, all claim to be conservatives.

They defile the honorable philosophy of conservatism with that claim as thoroughly as the Communists defile the honorable philosophy of liberalism.

I sympathize with some of my constituents who are honestly bewildered and confused by the trash of the rightwing extremists.

I even feel sympathetic with those who have been taken in as dupes.

But I have nothing but seething contempt for the originators of the hoaxes and swindles, from the ludicrous leaders of the Birch Society to the equally ludicrous director of the Cinema Educational Guild, including any and all of the several hundred similar self-styled patriotic groups.

They are anything but patriotic. Indeed, a good case can be made that they are unpatriotic, and downright un-American. For they are doing a devil's work far better than Communists themselves could do.

It is curious to me that they all have generally the same aims, issued in all out, uncompromising, almost hysterical demands: Get the United States out of the U.N. Stop all foreign aid. Repeal the income tax. Abandon NATO and bring our troops home from Europe.

It is ironic that these very aims are very likely identical to the real hopes and aspirations of the Kremlin.

At any rate, I could not imagine a program that would delight Khrushchev more.

For we have a United Nations, with imperfections to be sure, but a U.N. in which the Soviet Union has had to resort to a veto on 100 occasions, while we have never had to resort to a veto at all. We have a United Nations which the Soviet Premier has bitterly attacked on numerous occasions as U.S. controlled. A United Nations the Communists have never been able to control or subvert to their own use.

Yet, say the extremists, abandon it to the Communists.

Stop all foreign aid, the self-styled patriots say. Not some, not most, but all: military and economic. Let us stop helping to maintain 2 million free world troops on the perimeter of the Soviet Union, the patriots are really demanding. Let us write off every nation of the world as unrestricted fair game for the Communists, they are really saying. And if these countries need help in establishing military, and political and economic stability, let the Communists, or somebody else, provide it, they are really saying.

Repeal the income tax, they say. Not cut taxes, repeal them. And repeal our national defense, in the process.

Abandon NATO, they say. For the Birch leader has said:

With regard to that brainchild of Dean Acheson, godchild of Harry Truman, and eventual ward of Dwight Eisenhower, we have repeatedly insisted for years that it was probably the biggest—and certainly one of the most expensive—hoax in all human history.

Abandon NATO, they say—and leave Europe to the whim or mercy of the Soviet Union.

It is an amazing paradox that the rightwing extremists find the same programs and organizations to be subversive that the leftwing extremists find to be the "tools and weapons of the Wall Street imperialists," as witness Communist Party literature on our mutual security programs and NATO.

Of late I have been receiving letters from Birchers and their fellow travelers calling for removal of American troops in Vietnam. And I have also been receiving letters from Communists, leftwingers, and their fellow travelers calling for precisely the very same thing.

No, much as the fright peddlers, the rightwing extremists, and the Communists may desire such mutual goals, America is not going to bow to their dictates.

Let us, by all means, debate, as reasonable and rational and realistic people, the successes and failures of the United Nations and foreign aid·

But let us not do it on the basis of childish slogans or on the inane promise that they are Communist programs adopted by a Communist or pro-Communist Government in Washington.

Our policies—American policies—are open to question and debate—as they must always be.

I am a Republican—and I shall continue to question the cold-war policies of a Democratic administration and fight those I consider unwise.

But both political parties—Republicans and Democrats—have the best interests of the country we love in mind and heart.

I wonder, however, about the fright peddlers and the followers of an organization whose founder has declared: "Democracy is merely a deceptive phrase, a weapon of demagoguery and a perennial fraud."

Clutching at half-truths and downright falsehoods, the fright peddlers fabricate hoaxes, as we have seen, which frighten Americans and divert their attention from the real menace. They sow suspicion and hatred. They attempt to undermine faith in Government, its institutions, and its leaders. They preach resistance to the laws of our land. They degrade America and Americans, and do it as well as—or better than—the Communists do.

Yet, their followers—and even some honest conservatives—continually ask me: Why do I keep berating them, instead of the Communists?

I loathe and despise communism and Communists. By voice and by vote, all of my adult life I have attacked them and opposed them.

I expect the hoaxes and the spreading of hysteria, the sowing of suspicion, and the denigration of our Government, institutions, and leaders from the camp of the enemy, communism, but not from fellow Americans.

I shall always fight the big lie, the smear, witch hunts, anti-Catholicism, anti-Semitism, racism of any kind—which are not the hallmarks of conservatism, but are the trademarks of communism and fascism.

I am concerned about rightwing extremists, not because of the noise they make, which, as with the vile Communists, is out of proportion to their size. I am concerned because they are, after all, Americans, not agents sworn to allegiance to a foreign power.

Astonishingly to me, I sometimes get letters from avowed Birchers who furiously deny their leader has ever charged the Central Intelligence Agency is Communist controlled, or that Dulles was a Communist, or that NATO is a Communist planned hoax.

And I find it equally hard to believe that the followers of the fright peddlers are all wholly oblivious to the anti-Semitism, anti-Catholicism, and outright racism of many of their "saviors."

I am going to read a letter of the kind which arrives now and again. I cite the letter not to "prove" that all rightwing extremists are bigots or that a majority are; I really do not know how many are, perhaps very few.

I cite it merely to show that this type of person, the follower of Myron Fagan and Gerald L. K. Smith, has often found a new, "respectable" home in an extremist rightwing group that denies being bigoted.

The letter, from Westminster, Calif., reads in part:

Sirs: I am writing you again just to state that you can ignore me but you are sure not being ignored, your latest blast at Americans in the John Birch Society is just more evidence of your support of communism. I am a member of the Birch Society and I know many other members and every one of them are decent Americans who are interested in constitutional government and free enterprise and a real education for their children, and who mean to have it in spite of the grip that Jew communism that you support has on our country and Government. * * *

On this law by superior force that is called integration what do you think is going to be gained by that, the Jew press, radio, TV, and papers all scream the law of the land, who do you think believes it * * *. If you want integration let's start with the Jew schools. And synagogues * * *.

When are you going to stand up like a white man.

That is more than enough to illustrate my point—and to complete this autopsy.

My conclusion is simply this: Perhaps 10 percent of the 60,000 letters I receive each month fall into the category of fright mail.

This mail flies in the face of a clear, stern, and pertinent warning from a great and dedicated American, J. Edgar Hoover, in February 1962. Mr. Hoover then wrote in the Journal of the American Bar Association:

Today, far too many self-styled experts on communism are plying the highways of America, giving erroneous and distorted information. This causes hysteria, false alarms, misplaced apprehension by many of our citizens. We need enlightenment about communism but this information must be factual, accurate and not tailored to echo personal idiosyncrasies. To quote an old aphorism: We need more light and less heat.

Can these cruelly swindled victims of the fright peddlers be shocked into a reappraisal of their swindlers and be reclaimed as valuable and effective contributors in the fight against the real enemy? I do not know. But I believe it is time such an attempt be made.

Perhaps I am naive about this. Yet I feel there must be some—and they belong to both political parties—who can be persuaded to join the ranks again of sensible and decent anti-Communist, pro-Americans devoted to defending our Nation against defilement of both the extreme left and extreme right, here and abroad.

America has enough immediate and deadly dangerous enemies, without manufacturing hobgoblins. America can use all the responsible help it can receive.

INDEX

INDEX